SIMPLE OPTIONS INVESTING

(Small Investment & Fast Profits).

The Easy Trading Course

By Shawn Wilkinson
Copyright 2014 Shawn Wilkinson

Book cover design by: Jordan Escoto

~~~

Index of Chapters:

CHAPTER #1:

Part#1: Purpose & History.

Part#2: Great Home Based Business.

Part#3: Why you should take this Course.

Part#4: Index of Chapters

CHAPTER #2: Options vs. Stocks.

CHAPTER #3: What are Stock Options?

CHAPTER #4: Option Chains.

CHAPTER #5: ITM vs OTM.

CHAPTER #6: STOCK CRITERIA, WATCHLIST & QUOTE

CHAPTER #7: Candlesticks & Studies.

CHAPTER #8: Charts: Buy/Sell Indicators.

CHAPTER #9: Money Management Guidelines.

CHAPTER #10: Which Options To Buy?

Part #1: Quick Profit Estimating w/Buy & Sell charts/chains.

Part #2: Daily, 5 Min. & full day Charts Analysis.

Part #3: 20 Min. trade charts & chains.

Part #4: Daily Chart reversal; Trade w/6 Time lapse Min. charts.

Part #5: Quick trades w/charts & chains.

CHAPTER #11: Using Stops.

CHAPTER #12: Part #7: Paper Trading & Tool.

CHAPTER #13: Part #8: Summary.

CHAPTER #1

Course Purpose & History

If you have never invested in the stock market, or, if you are already an investor, this Educational Course will teach you how to start your own home business with very little money, and how to become a successful stock option investor.

The initial idea of the Author was to find a SIMPLE trading strategy risking small investments, and making quick, consistent profits; investing either part-time or full time from the home. However, educational material for this specific type of investing was not found. As such, the SOI trading strategy had to be developed. Countless hours over months were spent in trial and error investing, to develop this simple, successful trading strategy presented here.

The author is not a stock broker. He has never been a stock broker. He does not manage or invest money for other people. He is an independent stock option investor. He developed what this course teaches. He invests his money using the very same, simple, successful trading strategy you have the opportunity to learn, and use.

THREE GOALS OF THIS COURSE

This stock option investing course was developed with three goals in mind: 1) keep it simple enough for anybody to understand and use; 2) make sure an investor with as little as $500 could start trading; 3) make sure the trading strategy, when followed, made money for the investor. This stock option investing course achieves all three goals.

The author is proud to offer this educational course on stock option investing. This course is simple to learn, simple to use, and easy to be successful with.

GREAT HOME BASED BUSINESS

This Course offers you the educational material and tools necessary to start your own home based business as an independent investor. There are some great advantages of this Home Business, besides the obvious one of working for yourself.

(a). Economical start-up cost: new traders have opened a broker account with as little as $500.

(b). High Profit Potential: look at the two worksheets which follow (g), one for 1 week of trades, the 2nd for 1 month of trades. Take note of the % of profit for the risk amount.

(c). Limited losses: with a cash account you cannot lose more than the amount of money you invest in each trade. More importantly, if you follow the guidelines in Chapter #9, any loss should be minimal. Take note of the 3 losses (in red) in the two worksheets.

(d). No competition or clients: you don't compete against another business offering the same products or services, and you don't have to rely on clients. The only determining factor for success is your ability to execute the Trade Strategy.

(e). Mobile access: Every day the stock market is open, your business is open, regardless of where you might be as long as you have access to the internet during market hours.

(f). Work minutes or hours: you'll notice many of the trade examples in the Course are for periods of 15 to 20 minutes. After you make 1 trade for the day and are satisfied with the amount of profit you made, you can take off the rest of the day. Hey, you're the boss.

(g). No vendors or supply problems: every day there are more trade opportunities than a person can execute. The key is to have a Trading Strategy which narrows down the number of stocks to watch, and, makes it easy for you to recognize Buy and Sell indicators when they happen. Which is exactly what the SOI will teach you to do.

We are going to look at a copy of 1 week of trades made by an independent Stock Option Investor, applying the very same trading strategy contained in this course.

WORKSHEET #1

1 Week of Trades:

DATE	STK SYM	STK PRICE	BUY/SELL	OPTION	EXPIRE	PRICE	#CTRCTS	AP/AR INCL FEE	TRADE+/-	INV.FUND $500	FUND +/-
Mon7/08	AAPL	416.2	BUY	PUT 400	JY/12th	$0.62	4	($261)			
Mon7/08		411.9	SELL			$1.27	4	$495	$234	$734	$234
Mon7/08	QCOM	60.6	BUY	PUT 60	JY/12th	$0.32	6	($207)			
Mon7/08		60	SELL			$0.53	6	$303	$96	$830	$330
Tue7/09	AAPL	413.2	BUY	CALL 430	JY/12th	$0.27	10	($278)			
Tue7/09		422.3	SELL			$1.18	10	$1,162	$884	$1,714	$1,214
Tue7/09	NFLX	241.4	BUY	CALL 250	JY/12th	$1.26	2	($264)			
Tue7/09		245.8	SELL			$2.66	2	$520	$256	$1,970	$1,470
Wed7/10	LNKD	191	BUY	CALL 195	JY/12th	$1.07	2	($226)			
Wed7/10		190.5	SELL			$0.82	2	$152	($74)	$1,896	$1,396
Wed7/10	LNKD	190.5	BUY	PUT 185	JY/12th	$0.62	5	($324)			
Wed7/10		187.7	SELL			$0.94	5	$456	$132	$2,028	$1,528
Wed7/10	AMZN	290.4	BUY	CALL 295	JY/12th	$0.80	4	($333)			
Wed7/10		292.2	SELL			$1.18	4	$459	$126	$2,154	$1,654
Fri7/12	LNKD	197.2	BUY	CALL 200	JY/12th	$0.45	5	($239)			
Fri7/12		200	SELL			$0.95	5	$461	$221	$2,375	$1,875
Fri7/12	NFLX	251	BUY	CALL 255	JY/12th	$0.50	5	($264)			
Fri7/12		253.2	SELL			$1.10	5	$536	$272	$2,647	$2,147

1 WEEK 9 TRADES RISK HIGH:$333 RISK LOW:$207 8 GAINS 1 LOSS TTL:+$2147

IMPORTANT: the most amount of money put at risk, thus, the most amount of money which could have been lost, was $333 on Wed. 7/10. The average profit per trade was $238. Of the 9 trades made in the week, 1 trade lost money, also on Wed. 7/10. The amount lost was only $74 because the Money Management Guidelines (Chapter #9), were followed.

Next is a copy of 1 month of trades made by a different independent Stock Option Investor, applying the very same trading strategy contained in this course.

WORKSHEET #2: 1 Month of Trades:

Date	Symbol	Cost	#cntrcts	Risk Amt	Sell	Rtn Amt	Loss/Gain	%	500 Fund
2 Oct.	AAPL	4.15	1	415	4.95	495	58	20	558
3 Oct.	AAPL	1.73	2	346	2.95	590	221	70	779
4 Oct.	AAPL	1.33	3	399	2.3	690	265	72	1044
7 Oct.	AAPL	3	1	300	4	400	78	33	1122
8 Oct.	AMZN	4.15	1	415	8.45	845	408	103	1530
8 Oct.	LNKD	3.8	1	380	9.4	940	588	147	2118
9 Oct.	NFLX	2.43	2	486	5.96	1192	683	145	2801
11 Oct.	FB	1.21	4	484	1.5	600	90	23	2891
14 Oct.	AAPL	2.18	2	436	1.99	398	60	14	2831
15 Oct.	LNKD	3.2	1	320	3.75	375	33	17	2864
16 Oct.	BAC	0.52	8	416	0.67	536	94	28	2958
18 Oct.	GOOG	3.3	1	330	5.5	550	198	66	3156
18 Oct.	AAPL	0.7	6	420	1.06	636	171	46	3327
21 Oct.	AAPL	2.8	1	280	3.55	355	53	25	3380
21 Oct.	TSLA	1.86	2	372	2.75	550	155	47	3535
22 Oct.	NFLX	1.98	2	396	3.05	610	211	53	3746
22 Oct.	IBM	0.83	5	415	1.02	510	67	16	3813
23 Oct.	BA	0.9	5	450	0.8	400	90	20	3723
23 Oct.	GS	0.43	10	430	0.5	500	35	16	3758
24 Oct.	AAPL	1.85	2	370	3.55	710	318	85	4076
24 Oct.	GOOG	2.1	2	420	2.8	560	137	32	4213
28 Oct.	FB	2.29	2	458	2.88	576	95	20	4308
29 Oct.	NFLX	1.7	2	340	3.9	780	417	129	4725
30 Oct.	NFLX	1.45	3	435	1.79	537	87	20	4812
31 Oct.	AAPL	1	4	400	1.67	668	242	67	5054
31 Oct.	PCLN	1.8	2	360	2.45	490	107	29	5161

26 TRADES: Avg. Risk 395   TOTAL PROFIT: $4661   Avg. Trade Profit: 179

Notice this worksheet for an entire month had only 26 trades. The most money risked was $450 on Oct. 23. The profit average per trade was $179. Note the 2 losses: 1 for $60 on Oct. 14th, and the other for $90 on Oct. 23rd. Again, following the very crucial Money Management Guidelines (Chapter

#9), both losses were far less than the average profit per trade.

Why You Should Take This Course

#1. Great Home Based Business Opportunity.

#2. Material is presented in a simple, understandable way, easy to learn and use.

#3. The Course is a great value, far less than the average profit of 1 trade.

#4. You'll learn how to "paper trade" for free BEFORE you open a broker account.

#5. You can apply the trading strategy to options or stocks.

Congratulations on taking a step toward working for yourself and achieving financial success.

CHAPTER #2

Options Instead Of Stocks

Why stock options instead of stocks?

#1. ECONOMICS! ECONOMICS! ECONOMICS!

Stock options offer a greater opportunity for quicker profits with less capital than stocks.

Here is an Example based upon a real trade: We both have a $500 investment fund.

Fri. 5/24: MSFT (Microsoft) stock price is at $34 a share.

You Buy 14 shares of stock @ $34 each for a total risk of $476.

SOI buyS 6 Call Options: Strike Price 34, Expiration 6/22, @ $.75 each: risk of $450: (option contract is 100 shares, so the cost would be 600 x .75).

Tues. 5/28 MSFT is trading for $35 a share:

You can sell your 14 shares @ $35: Gain $14 (3%).

SOI sells the 6 Call Options @ $1.35 each: Gain $360 (80%).

Risking approx. the same amount of money, and even though the stock gained $1 vs. the options gain of $.60, the options made $346 MORE than the stock investment. Why? Because the Options traded the equivalent of 600 shares vs. the 14 shares you bought.

You would have had to Buy approx. 360 shares at $34 each, for an investment of over $12,000, to make the same $360 profit the Options made with just $450!

NOTE: If MSFT gained 5% EVERY month, it would take you approx. 12 months to make the extra $346 the options made in 3 days. MSFT gained over 10% the 12 months between 7/'12 – 06/'13.

The Options Risk: MSFT closed @ $33 on 6/21. If you still own your shares, you have a loss of only $14, and do not have to sell unless you want to. If I do not sell the Options by market close on 6/21, (or don't "exercise"), they become worthless for a loss of $450. HOWEVER, the options were sold on 5/28 for a $346 profit.

The SOI trading strategy is to make, and take quick profits.

NOTE: MSFT on Tue., Nov. 12th traded for $37.60. Your $476 investment would be worth approx. $526, for a profit of $50 in a little more than 5 months.

#2: MAKING A PROFIT WHEN A STOCK GOES UP OR DOWN

With the SOI trading strategy you can make money if the market goes up or down. Here is an example of making money when the market is going down:

AMZN (Amazon) on Nov. 1st started trading at $363 and at 10:00 a.m. had dropped to about $361. If you owned AMZN stock you would have been losing money. At 10:00 5 Put (wanting the stock to go down) Options, Strike Price 360 were bought at $0.84 for a Risk of $420.

The 5 Options were sold at approx.10:15, for $1.56 and a $320 (73%) profit in 15 MINUTES. The stock price dropped over $2 a share and the Options gained $0.72.

Buying Put Options is not the only way to make money when a stock goes down. You can "short" the stock itself and make money if the stock price goes down. For you to have made the same $320, you would have had to sell approximately 160 shares of stock, which means you would have had to have over $57,000 equity in your account, or been approved for that much credit.

Would you rather risk $57,000 to make $320, or risk $420 to make $320?

Anybody can learn, and trade the SOI way. This successful trading strategy is simple to understand and use. Take a step toward becoming a successful,

Home Business, independent market investor by taking the rest of the Options Course.

CHAPTER #3

What Are Stock Options?

For this Course we are only talking about Equity (Stock) Options.

A stock option is the RIGHT, but NOT obligation, to either BUY or SELL a specific amount of underlying stock, for a specific price before an expiration date. A single option standard contract equals 100 shares of the underlying stock.

There are two basic kinds of Stock Options: CALLS and PUTS.

The Option to BUY stock at a contracted price is a CALL. The Option to SELL stock at a contracted price is a PUT.

CALL UP: PUT DOWN.

If you think the stock is going up, like the MSFT example in Seg. #2, you buy CALL (UP) Options. If you think the stock is going down, like the AMZN example in Seg. #2, you buy PUT (DOWN) Options.

Call and Put Options share basic components:

#1. Expiration Date: the date on which the Option expires. If an Option is not sold or exercised by the expiration date, the Option becomes worthless.

#2. Strike Price: (Also known as Exercise Price): The price at which the option owner has the right to buy (CALL) or sell (PUT) the underlying stock. The

CALL in the MSFT example meant you had the right to BUY the stock (600 shares) at $34 no matter what the stock price was. If MSFT was up to $40, you could exercise the options and still buy MSFT for $34. Or you could SELL the Options.

The PUT in the AMZN example meant you had the right to SELL the stock (500shares at $360 no matter what the stock price was. If AMZN dropped to $355 you could exercise the options and still sell AMZN stock for $360. Or you could sell the Options.

Later on we will compare Selling Options for a profit vs Exercising the Options.

#3. Premium: the price for the Option. Premiums are NOT fixed or refundable, and are subject to market volatility. NOTE: if the Premium is $1, the price of the Option standard contract is $100 ($1 x 100 shares multiplier).

#4. IN THE MONEY: CALL: Value of stock is ABOVE strike price. If MSFT is at $35, a $34 Call Option is IN THE MONEY. PUT: current value of stock is BELOW strike price. If AMZN is at $355, a $360 Put Option is IN THE MONEY. IN THE MONEY simply means if you Exercise your Option, you can Buy or Sell the stock for a profit.

#5. OUT OF THE MONEY: CALL: Strike price is ABOVE current stock price: MSFT is at $33, a $34 Call Option is OUT OF THE MONEY. PUT: Strike price BELOW current stock price: AMZN at $360, a $355 Put Option is OUT OF THE MONEY.

CHAPTER #4

Options Chains

An option chain is a list of the stock option contracts, and their data, available for a given stock. If you go to different sites for an option quote, you might find different Chain layouts, but all have the same basic information displayed.

Here is an IBM OPTIONS CHAIN:

In the Chain we see:

(H) The company name, date, and time.

(1) The stock symbol, IBM; the last price the STOCK traded for, $194; and how much the stock price has changed from the previous trading day: in this example the $194 is the same price IBM closed at the trading day before.

(2) Bid is what a buyer is offering to pay for 100 shares of stock. The Ask is the price a seller wants for 400 shares of stock. The volume is the number of shares traded.

(3) The chain is for Calls and Puts; the number of strike prices (chosen from a menu) to be displayed; and the contract type is standard (1 contract ='s 100 shares).

(4) These options expire July 20, '13 which is highlighted in blue. We can also choose to see options for any of the dates listed horizontally.

(5) Calls and (6) Puts are shown side-by-side separated by:

(7) The column of Strike Prices, in this case 11 different prices. The Strike/Exercise Price of an option is the "price" at which the stock can be bought (Call) or sold (Put).

(8),(8A) The Volume of how many option contracts were traded throughout the day. The more volume the easier it will be to trade the stock option.

(8B) Is the Open Interest which is the total number of option contracts still outstanding. These are contracts that have NOT been exercised, closed, or expired. The higher the open interest, the easier it will be to trade the stock option.

(9) The "Last Trade" column lists the last price the option was traded for (opened or closed); and the "$ Chng Cl" shows the change in the options price from the last traded price of the day before. The "Last Trade" could have been minutes or hours ago.

(10) The BID is the latest price a buyer is willing to PAY for that option. Many times when selling an option, the BID is the price received. The ASK (10) is the latest price a seller is willing to ACCEPT for that

option. Many times when buying an option, the ASK is the price paid.

In the next Lecture we are going to discuss ITM vs. OTM.

CHAPTER #5

In The Money Vs. Out Of The Money

We are going to use the same IBM CHAIN as in Chapter #4.

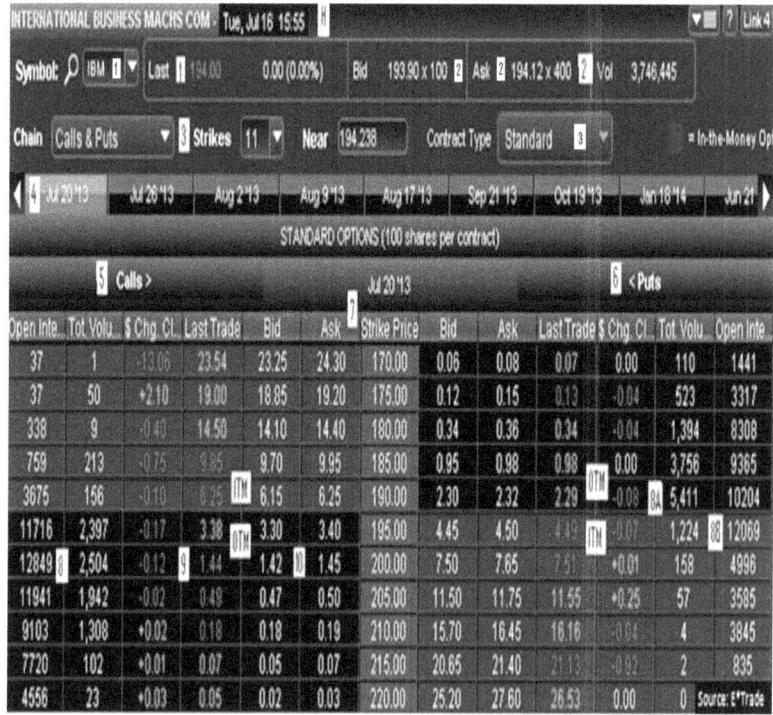

(ITM) means "In The Money". ITM for a CALL (blue highlight) means the current value of the stock is ABOVE the strike price. If you own 1 IBM July/20 Call-190, you could Exercise the Option and BUY 100 Shares of IBM Stock for just $190 each, even though the stock is worth $194 each. Thus, the Option @ SP $190 is ITM.

REMEMBER: a CALL PREMIUM only has to be equal to, or greater than the STOCK PRICE MINUS the STRIKE PRICE. If the STOCK PRICE is 194, and the STRIKE PRICE is 190, then the PREMIUM MUST be at least $4., which is INTRINSIC VALUE.

To Buy the CALL-190 Option at Ask would cost $6.25 even though the Stock is only worth 194. The cost of $6.25 is $4 INTRINSIC VALUE (194 - 190), and $2.25 TIME VALUE (in addition to INTRINSIC) which is more than what the stock can be bought for if the Option is exercised. Remember, buying a CALL speculates the STOCK & OPTION PRICE WILL GO UP BEFORE THE OPTION EXPIRES.

(OTM) means "Out of The Money". OTM for a CALL means the current value of the stock is BELOW the strike price. If you held 1 IBM July/20 Call-195, you could Exercise the Option and BUY 100 Shares of IBM Stock for $195 each, even though the stock is only worth $194 each. Thus, the Option @ $195 is OTM.

(ITM) for a PUT (blue highlight) means the current value of the stock is BELOW the Strike Price. If you held 1 IBM July/20 Put-195, you could Exercise the Option and SELL 100 Shares of IBM Stock for $195 each, even though the stock is worth $194 each. Thus, the Option @ $195 is ITM.

REMEMBER: a PUT PREMIUM only has to be equal to, or greater than the STRIKE PRICE MINUS the STOCK PRICE. If the STOCK PRICE is 194, and the STRIKE PRICE is 195, then the PREMIUM MUST be at least $1.00 (INTRINSIC VALUE).

To Buy the PUT-195 Option at Ask would cost $4.50 even though the Stock is worth 194. The Premium of $4.50 has a $1 INTRINSIC VALUE (195 – 194), and a $3.50 TIME VALUE cost above what the stock can be SOLD for if the Option is exercised. Buying a PUT is speculating the STOCK and OPTION PRICE WILL GO DOWN BEFORE THE OPTION EXPIRES.

(OTM) for a PUT means the current value of the stock is ABOVE the Strike Price. If you own 1 IBM July 20 Put-190, you could Exercise the Option and SELL 100 Shares of IBM Stock for $190 each, even though the stock is worth $194 each. Thus, the Option @ $190 is OTM.

When Buying an Option, the amount of INTRINSIC VALUE vs. TIME VALUE is a very crucial factor. For example: with IBM @ $194, if you Buy a Call-195 @ $3.40, the Strike Price is OTM, and the Premium cost is all TIME VALUE. If the stock price DOES NOT increase by expiration, the TIME VALUE will become worthless.

If at expiration IBM stock is at 194, even the Call-190 @ $6.25 will lose its' TIME VALUE and only be worth $4.00: CALL Strike Price (190) PLUS the Premium (4) must be EQUAL TO, or GREATER THAN the stock price: 194 = 190 + 4. However, if IBM stock rises to $200 before the expiration date, the Call-190 MUST be worth at least $10: 200 = 190 + 10.

Option INTRINSIC VALUE is moved by the true value of stock. TIME VALUE is speculative, driven by supply and demand, and stock volatility, which brings us to the next segment, Stock criteria for buying options.

CHAPTER #6

Stock Criteria, Watchlist & Quote

Since STOCK OPTIONS are based upon an underlying stock, Option prices usually move the same direction the stock moves. As such, our method of trading options is based upon certain stock criteria.

STOCK CRITERIA

a). DAILY VOLUME AVERAGE: usually stocks trading more than 500,000 shares a day. Greater volume = greater stock and option volatility.

b). VOLATILITY: due to short term trading, a stock needs to move in price (gain/loss) at least 10%, (or 5% on high $ stocks), 2-3 times every 60 trade days. Volatility equals good chart trends.

VOLATILITY CHART

The Chart below shows the approximate % of price moves over a 100 day period. The %'s represent the approximate move from the previously marked %. Obviously, this Stock meets our criteria.

BAC Criteria Chart Example:

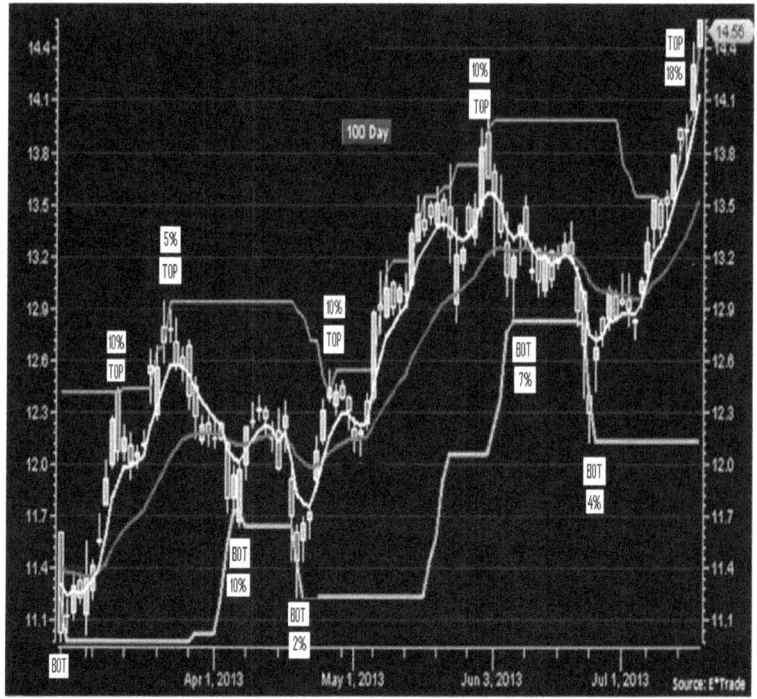

c). CHART TREND: we prefer stocks with multiple tops and bottoms. The Chart above shows many tops and bottoms, which created very good trends and trade opportunities. Let's take a moment and look at a couple of these.

d). OPTION VOLUME: the Volume of Options traded for a specific strike price must be enough to generate volatility. Volume is found on the Option Chain below. Also note the Open Interest, which is the number of outstanding contracts for each strike price.

| Jul 20 '13 | Jul 26 '13 | Aug 2 '13 | Aug 9 '13 | Aug 17 '13 | Sep 21 '13 | Oct 19 '13 | Jan 18 '14 | Jun 21 |

STANDARD OPTIONS (100 shares per contract)

< Calls >					Jul 20 '13	< Puts >				
Open Inte.	Tot.Volu.	$ Chg. Cl.	Last Trade	Bid	Ask	Strike Price	Bid	Ask	Last Trade	$ Chg. Cl.	Tot.Volu.	Open Inte.
37	1	-13.00	23.54	23.25	24.30	170.00	0.06	0.08	0.07	0.00	110	1441
37	50	+2.10	19.00	18.85	19.20	175.00	0.12	0.15	0.13	-0.04	523	3317
338	9	-0.40	14.50	14.10	14.40	180.00	0.34	0.36	0.34	-0.04	1,394	8308
759	213	-0.75	9.85	9.70	9.95	185.00	0.95	0.98	0.98	0.00	3,756	9365
3675	156	-0.19	6.25 ITM	6.15	6.25	190.00	2.30	2.32	2.29 OTM	-0.06	5,411 OA	10204
11716	2,397	-0.17	3.38 ITM	3.30	3.40	195.00	4.45	4.50	4.45 ITM	-0.07	1,224	12069
12849	2,504	-0.12	1.44	1.42	1.45	200.00	7.50	7.65	7.51	+0.01	158	4996
11941	1,942	-0.02	0.49	0.47	0.50	205.00	11.50	11.75	11.55	+0.25	57	3585
9103	1,308	+0.02	0.18	0.18	0.19	210.00	15.70	16.45	16.16	-0.04	4	3845
7720	102	+0.01	0.07	0.05	0.07	215.00	20.65	21.40	21.13	-0.52	2	835

e). WEEKLY OPTIONS: not all stocks have weekly expiring options. Many still only offer monthly expiration dates (3rd Sat. of each month). We prefer the weekly options because they are more economical (less Time Value).

Because there are thousands of stocks to watch, it is necessary to create a short Watchlist of stocks which meet our criteria. An actual OPTIONS WATCHLIST of 24 stocks is below. The List also includes the 3 big Markets (1).

WATCHLIST:

▲ Symbol	Last Trade	$ Chg. Close	% Chg. Close	High	Low	Tot. Volume
$COMPX	3,452.13	+28.57	+0.83	3,468.56	3,436.34	0
$DJI	15,179.85	+109.67	+0.73	15,261.71	15,078.71	0
$SPX	1,639.04	+12.31	+0.76	1,646.50	1,630.34	0
AAPL	431.90	+1.85	+0.43	435.70	430.3615	9,264,955
AMZN	278.22	+4.23	+1.54	280.20	275.65	2,885,580
BAC	13.22	+0.15	+1.15	13.2617	13.13	115,503,854
BBRY	14.28	-0.16	-1.11	14.65	14.18	12,319,558
BIDU	96.33	-1.67	-1.70	99.00	96.15	3,890,301
C	49.37	+0.15	+0.30	50.39	49.05	33,128,975
CF	184.88	+0.32	+0.17	185.8799	183.50	882,371
CME	76.39	+2.10	+2.83	76.68	74.46	3,260,184
CMG	367.68	-0.44	-0.12	372.11	365.00	257,156
CRM	38.24	+0.68	+1.81	38.82	37.08	6,542,552
FAS	65.97	+1.68	+2.61	66.81	64.97	6,503,249
FB		+0.33	+1.40	24.25	23.75	33,645,249
FFIV	74.53	+0.54	+0.73	75.31	74.05	1,180,915
GLD	133.77	-0.66	-0.49	134.0599	133.5201	4,072,812
GMCR	79.41	+1.03	+1.31	80.93	78.87	2,956,228
GOOG	886.50	+11.46	+1.31	889.43	878.28	2,146,638
GS	164.20	+1.28	+0.79	165.67	162.905	2,628,140
IBM	203.04	+0.84	+0.42	205.1713	202.55	3,220,009
LNKD	177.59	-0.65	-0.36	180.00	175.53	1,655,713
MA	578.19	+7.03	+1.23	580.98	574.07	724,717
MCD	98.74	+0.32	+0.33	99.69	98.301	4,885,470
NFLX	229.40	+15.41	+7.20	230.4999	223.75	5,122,192
PCLN	825.54	+9.79	+1.20	831.09	818.6005	822,413
WYNN	138.39	+3.25	+2.40	140.25	136.11	2,189,504

Source: E*Trade

The headers, "Last Trade", etc., are from a menu list and can be customized and arranged in different orders. The data constantly changes during the trading session and in this case, represents the closing numbers for the day of trading.

The first thing to note is the volume column. All of the stocks traded at least 500,000 shares with the exception of CMG. In some cases, the amount of shares traded is higher or lower than their daily average over 3 months. Remember: heavy trading volume means better volatility.

The "$ Chg. Close" column is the stock price gain or loss from the close of the previous trading day. The "% Chg. Close" column is the % of change the "$ Chg." represents.

Note the "% Chg. Close" column vs. the High-Low range (2). Even though CMG only changed -0.44 (-0.12%) for the day, it had a High-Low range of $7.11 (almost 2%) for the day, which is good price volatility, and makes up for the lack of volume.

Also, look at LNKD: it lost .65 for the day, not necessarily impressive for a stock price of $177. However, it had a High-Low range of $4.47 which is good volatility.

STOCK QUOTE

One way to determine if a stock meets the criteria is to look at the stock quote. Even though quotes are displayed differently, they contain a lot of the same data. Here is a typical stock quote.

COMPANY: OC

Symbol................OC (1)

Close..................28.71 (2)

Previous Close........27.59 (4)

Change................+1.12 (3)

Chg. Percent +4.10% (5)

Open..................27.69 (6)

Day's High............28.72 (7)

Day's Low.............27.69 (8)

Volume................3.63 Mil. (9)

Avg Vol 12 wks........7.65 Mil. Per day (10)

Bid.......................28.70 (11)

Ask......................28.78 (12)

52 Wk High 33.25 (13)

52 Wk Low........... 17.15 (14)

The stock quote above shows the following: The Company's symbol is OC (1). Current price of a share is $28.71(2), which is $1.12(3) more than the closing price of $27.59(4) of the day before. The $1.12 equals a 4.10%(5) gain of the price.

The "open" price of the day was $27.69(6), with a day's price high of $28.72(7), and price low of $27.69(8).

The day's volume was 3.63(9) million shares, well below the average daily volume over 12 weeks of 7.65(10) million shares.

The BID is $28.70(11), the ASK is $28.78(12). The 52 wk high is $33.25(13); 52 wk low is $17.15(14).

Based on the avg. daily volume, the High-Low 52 wk range (approx. 90%), and a one day gain over 4%, this stock qualifies as a good Options candidate. However, we now have to go to the Charts and Chains to make sure.

Going to the Option Chains would be the quickest next step. At the very least, we want 3 different Strike Prices for the same stock with at least 100 contracts volume each. Again, more volume usually means greater volatility.

If all qualifies at this point we now face the big question: what will the chart show?

CHAPTER #7

Criteria Charts

Candlesticks

The charts below are candlestick charts using a DAILY time frame. Each candlestick shows the HIGH, OPEN, CLOSE, and LOW for the time frame. You will find variations of colors and even hollow bodies. There are websites which go into greater detail about analyzing candlesticks.

In the charts used here, a Green body is for a GAIN (higher close than open), and a Red body for a LOSS (lower close than open). Also considered are the lengths of the Shadows (resistance), and the size of the Body compared to the Shadows and to other Bodies.

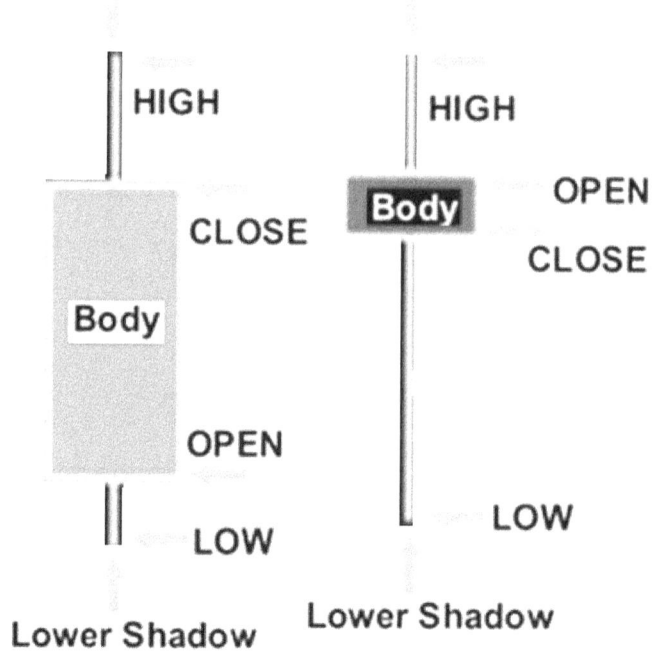

Ex. CHART #1: IBM WITH NO STUDIES:

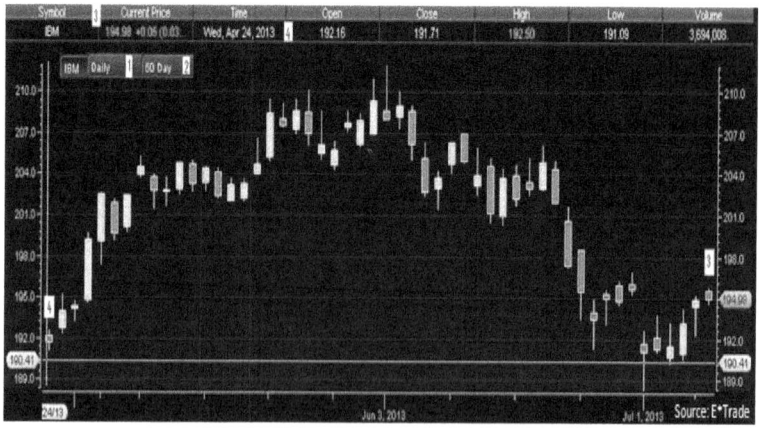

Chart #1 above shows a "Daily" time period (1); for 50 trading days (2); with current price and +/- for the day (July 8th)(3,3); and April 24 data is highlighted (4,4). Green sticks are gains, red are losses.

The highlighted time frame (4) defines the candlestick: Open(192.16), Close(191.71), High

(192.50), and Low(191.09). Between the High and Open is .34 which is represented by the Upper Shadow. Between the Low and Close is .62, which is represented by the Lower Shadow, and explains why the Upper Shadow is smaller than the Lower Shadow. The day closed only -.45 which is why the Body is Red and small on a grid of $3 increments.

Ex. CHART #2: IBM WITH STUDIES.

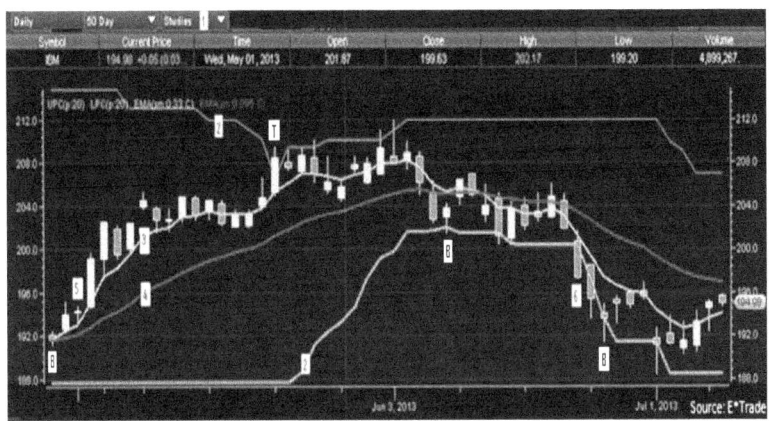

Chart #2 is for the same 50 days as #1 except using "Studies" (1) chosen from a menu: Price Channel (2)(green lines); a Moving Average of 5 periods (3)(yellow line), in this case days; and a Moving Average of 20 periods (4)(red line), also days. Decide which studies/indicators work for you.

Notice how the price channels make it easier to see tops (T)(chart highs), and bottoms (B)(chart lows). Also note in this chart, the increments are $4.

The 5 (yellow) vs. 20 (red) lines show where the 5 (short term) line crosses over, or crosses under ("Cross-Overs") the 20 (longer term) line. At (5 & 6), the 5MA line separates from the 20MA, which helps to validate trends and Buy/Sell indicators. We will cover Buy/Sell indicators later on.

In this case, we are looking to see if IBM meets the criteria listed in Part #6 for possible Options Trading. REMEMBER: for VOLATILITY the stock needs to move in price (gain/loss) at least 10%, (or 5% on high $ stocks), 2-3 times every 60 trade days; and for CHART TREND we prefer stocks with multiple tops and bottoms.

The chart increments are $4. From the very first Red stick at $192, to the stick on top of #3 at $204 is a $12 gain (5%+) in just 8 days. From $204 it gains another $5 in the next 11 days. From June 3rd at $208 it drops over $12 (red next to #6) in the next 15 days. IBM is more than Volatile enough for our criteria.

As for Chart Trends, we see 1 Top (T) and 3 Bottoms (B) in the 50 day time period. Multiple Tops/Bottoms are NOT a must in lieu of better than average volatility such as IBM. However, we PREFER multiple Tops/Bottoms because they are good indicators of resistance before a reversal, or before a breakout, which we will discuss later on. For right now, we are only concerned with the Chart Trends criteria.

B. Criteria Chart Ex. BAC

Below is a chart for BAC, also Daily time frames but for 100 days (1). This chart displays the same studies as IBM. From here on, all of the charts use the same studies unless otherwise noted. NOTE the CHART increments are only .30 due to the low price of the BAC stock. It is very important to ALWAYS be aware of the chart increments.

As before, we are interested to see if BAC Volatility and Chart Trends meet our criteria to trade options with. From #1 to #2 is approx. $1, a 9% move in 5 days. From #3 to #4 is approx. $1.30, a 10% move in 14 days. From #5 to #6 is approx. $1.60, a 12% move. Since the cross-over (7) on July 5th @ $13, BAC has gained $1.46 (11+%) through July 18th (8). There are also multiple tops and bottoms.

BAC more than meets our stock criteria. Do not overlook stocks based upon price.

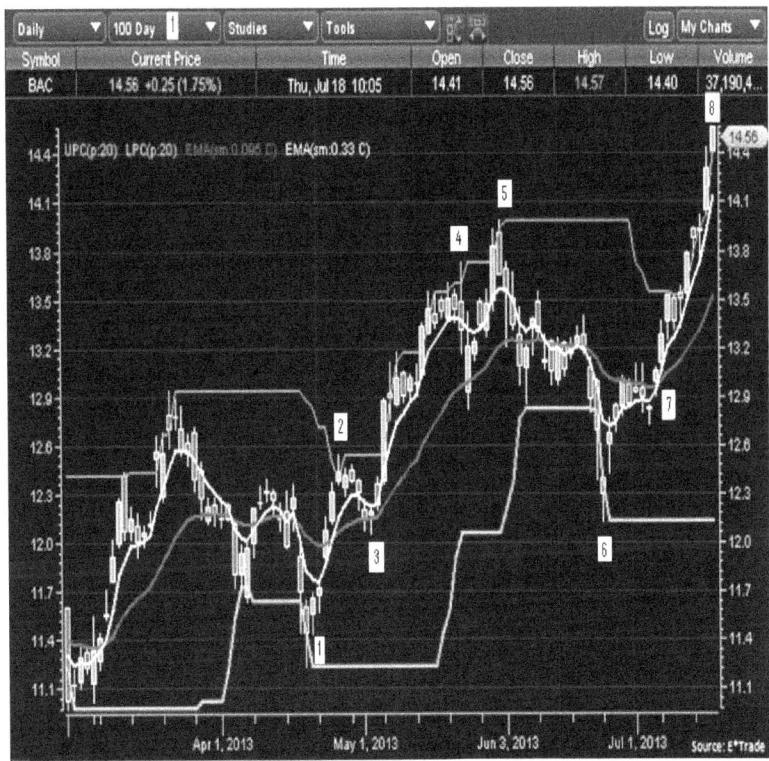

Charts Buy/Sell Indicators

Now that we basically know what stock options are, how they work, and how to qualify stocks for the trading strategy, the question is, how to make $$$. In order to make $$$, the first crucial question to be answered is:

WHEN TO BUY AND SELL?

Remember, we are using the same Studies as before. In the charts below you will learn how to determine what direction the stock will move, and when to buy or sell.

Ex. CHART: MSFT:

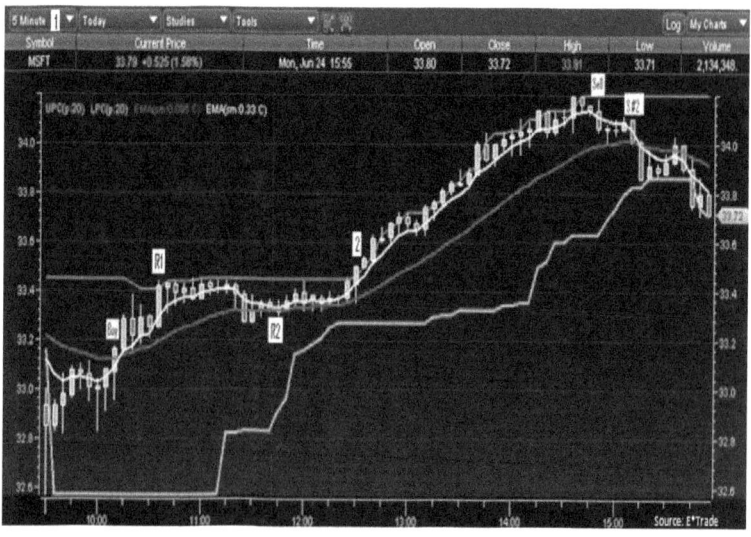

The MSFT chart above is for one day with "5 Minute" (1) time frames. The "Current Price" shows the gain of +0.525, and the % (1.58%) for the day from the previous close.

There is a $.07 difference in the price from the last price on the chart of $33.72 because there is "after market" trading on the stock which does not get displayed on the chart except under Current Price.

Under "Time" note the 15:55 time period for the final Red stick ending at $33.72 on the Chart which matches the "Close".

When the 5MA (yellow moving avg.) starts to cross over the 20MA (red) is a Buy (@ $33.20) Call signal. It is the 3rd gain in a row; all 3 sticks have lower SHADOWS showing resistance to going down; and there are no upper SHADOWS. The 2 Red (@ 09:50 & 09:55) have lower shadows, & their bodies did not go beneath the open @ 09:45 (4th time frame).

At 10:35 there is resistance (R1) at the upper price channel (green) for the stock to go any higher. At 11:35 (R2) there is resistance at the 20 MA for the stock not to go lower. Most IMPORTANTLY, R2 is still ABOVE the BUY point and ABOVE the 20MA.

At 2 there is a 2nd BUY indicator if the first is missed, which also acts as a strong "hold" indicator if already bought. Note the separation of the 5MA above the 20MA, and the push through the top price channel which has started to move up, also indicators.

At $34.10 (14:50) is the first SELL indicator. It is the 3rd Red stick in a row and is pushing BELOW 5MA, and BELOW the open of the Green @ 14:35. Also, the stock is up $0.90 (2.7%). If not SELL @ $34.10, a 2nd strong SELL (S#2) indicator is @ 15:10 and $34.

MSFT TRADE RESULTS

Remember, the trading strategy is to take quick profits. The actual Options trade results were: BUY JUNE 28 CALL-33.50 x 4 @ $.25: = RISK $113. All trade amounts include fees.

SELL @ .79 = 316 (Return) – 113 (Risk): = PROFIT OF + $190 (168%). NOTE: IF SELL @ S#2 (HIT R20):@$.72 = +$162. We'll discuss what option to buy later.

CHART AIG: (5 min 1 day):

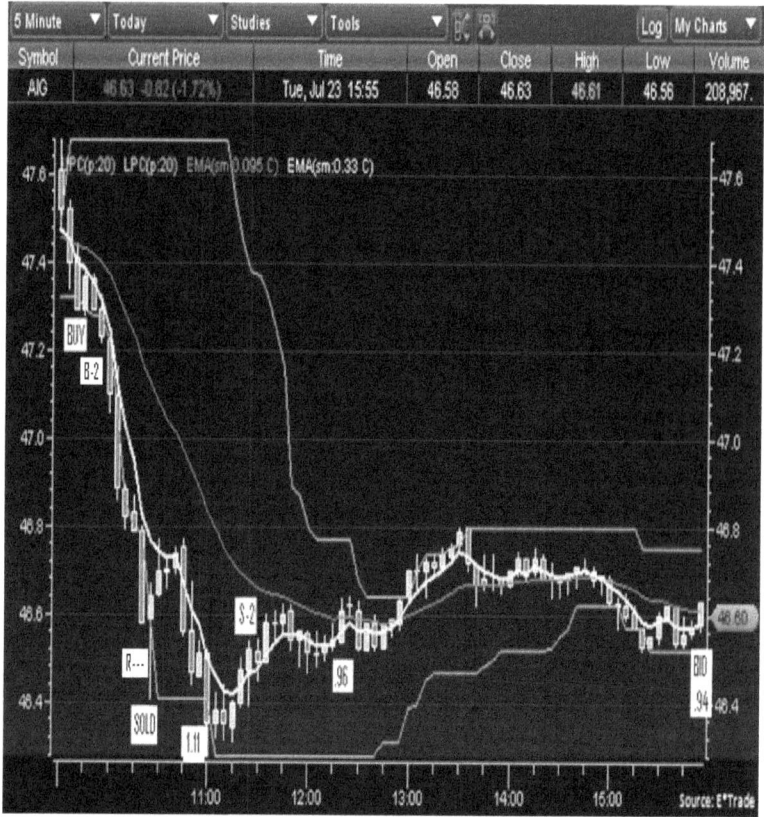

CHART AIG above has a strong BUY PUT signal: after jumping up at the open, it bounced back (long shadow) and headed down 3 consecutive Reds (5 min periods), thru the 20MA and below the 5MA (BUY). If the BUY was missed, a 2nd strong BUY signal was at 47.25 (B-2).

It might seem the Sell at $46.60 is very quick, especially since it is the first Green, and still under the 5MA. However, note the big resistance (R) bounce and the length of the lower shadow vs. body, which usually indicates a pending upward movement. Also, since the BUY, the stock has dropped over $0.70 (1.4%).

NOTE: had the Sell been at the very lowest point, approx. $46.34 @ 11:00 (1.11), the trade would have made $102 more. However, using the strategy of waiting until the stock had reversed over the 5MA to Sell, the Sell would have been at S2, making approx. $12 more for the trade. In hindsight, the Sell was a little quick, however, it is difficult to criticize a 92% profit!

AIG TRADE RESULTS

Remember, one of the keys to successful trading is being able to take a profit. The actual trade results were: BUY AIG PUT-47.50 @ $0.45 x6 = -$285 (Risk). SOLD @ $0.94 = $549 (Return) - $285 = +$264 (Profit @ 92%).

5 Min. Buy/Sell Chart

In the 1 Day, 5Min Chart below why is the Buy better at 2 than the 1? At the 1 the 5MA is still below the 20MA; it is the first body above both MA's; and though it did push through the new lower Upper Price Channel, it found Resistance at the previous Upper Price Channel level. At the 2 the 5MA is above the 20MA; it is the 2nd Green in a row above both MA's; and it has pushed through the new Upper Price Channel. Also note the lower shadows of the two sticks right before the Buy.

The SELL point is very good for a couple of reasons: 1) The option gain is right @ 26% (Buy @ 1.05 –

Sold @ 1.34); 2) previous stick has greater upper shadow resistance than lower resistance; 3) the red body is bigger than the previous green body; 4) upper shadow with no lower shadow. NOTE: if NOT sold here, and sold at 15:30 (last green above 5MA) the options would have sold for approx. .03 LESS.

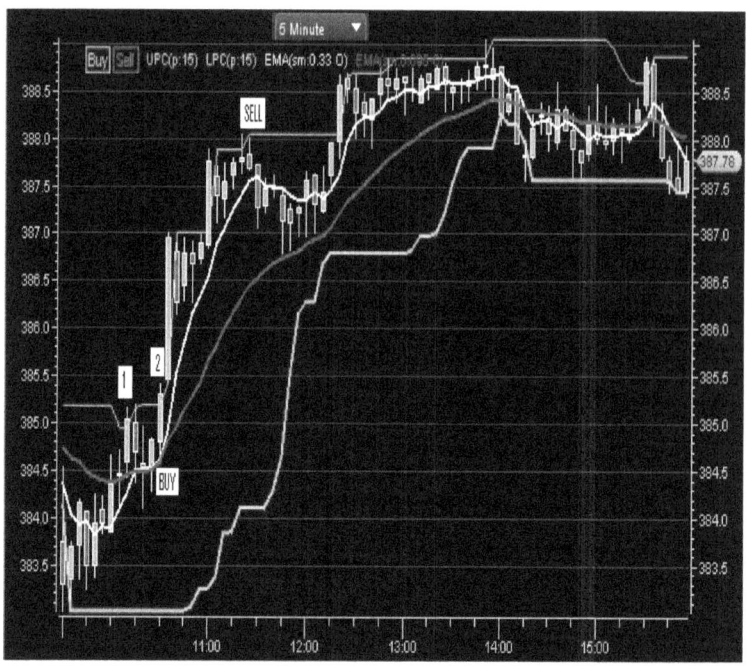

BUY/SELL CHART: GOOG

We're going to look at one more chart before moving on. The BUY indicator is very strong as it follows a 2nd cross-over of the 20MA by the 5MA. Note the increments of $2, thus, even if Resistance is met at the Upper Price Channel, there is enough room for the Option to move up or at least break even. The very next frame breaks through the Upper Price Channel and creates separation between the MA's.

The first Red at 13:05 is not a strong enough indicator to sell. However, the Red at 13:10 is a definite Sell, especially with the Option Profit dropping $.60. The trade results: Buy at $1.06 and Sell at $3.20 for a 200% profit.

KEY TO SUCCESS

FOLLOW THE TRADING STRATEGY. One of the common mistakes of traders is to look at a Sell, and notice, if they had NOT sold, even through a reversal, they would have eventually made more profit. Then they decide to change the Sell strategy, which often leads to profits turning into losses. The important question is whether or not the Sell point was good. If the Sell point was good, do not worry if you are leaving too much profit on the table.

Before moving on to which options to buy and making money, we are going to cover $$ Management keys.

CHAPTER #9

MONEY MANAGEMENT

One of the big reasons investors lose $$ is because they DO NOT follow a $$ Management Plan. Part of the OC trading strategy success is a result of employing the following $$ Mgmt plan.

The OC $ Management Plan has three parts:

a) Amount to invest.

b) Limiting A Loss.

c) Profit Target.

a) Amount to invest is usually determined by splitting the investment fund into 4 risk banks of 25% each. Starting with a fund of $5K there would be 4 banks of $1,250 each. As such, the entire fund is NOT put at risk in a single trade. Also, you have the ability to make more than one trade in a session.

Of course, if your initial fund is $1000, split it into just two risk banks of $500 each. You will notice the trade examples meet the criteria of a $1000 Investment Fund with two banks of $500.

Limiting A Loss

b) LIMITING A LOSS: Limit losses to approx. 25% depending on the type of trade and the amount at risk. If 25% of Fund is invested with a 25% loss, the total loss will be = to 6.25% of the Fund, which is acceptable. However, sometimes, you might need to exit the position even earlier. Don't stay in a losing position just because you have not lost 25%. Always follow the changing charts and indicators.

A simpler method of Stop Loss, which is very successful for new investors, is to set a limit on ANY loss depending on the amount of your I.F., such as:

I.F. is under $1000: NO Trade Loss OVER $100, which allows up to 9 Trades.
I.F. is $1K - 2K: NO Trade Loss OVER $150, which allows up to 13 Trades.
I.F. is $2K+: NO Trade Loss OVER $200, which guarantees at least 9 trades.

IMPORTANT: DO NOT stop limiting losses just because a previous loss eventually reversed and would have turned into a profit. The essential question is whether or not your Buy and Sell Points were good. There will be times when you follow the chart and make an excellent Buy, only to have the stock reverse immediately. Accept the limited Loss and move onto the next trade opportunity. If you start holding onto a loss beyond the Money Management recommendation, you will turn a small loss into a huge loss, and will not have the needed funds for the next trade opportunity.

REMEMBER: you only need a profit 60% of the time with the Trade Strategy.

KEY TO SUCCESS: A TRADER MUST KNOW HOW TO LIMIT A LOSS.

TAKE A PROFIT

c) TAKE A PROFIT: Set a Profit Target based on a 20% gain, or an actual money gain. Another constant mistake made by investors is NOT taking a profit, and then watching the profit turn into a loss.

Thus, when you do have a profit, it is crucial to also use a STOP LOSS to lock in and take a Profit. Here is a simple, successful strategy for Taking profits.

I.F. is under $1000: Trade Gain of $50+ CANNOT turn into a Trade LOSS.
I.F. is $1K - 2K - Trade Gain of $75 CANNOT go UNDER $50 Gain.
I.F. is $2K+: Trade Gain of $100 CANNOT go UNDER $75 Gain.

KEY TO SUCCESS: A TRADER MUST KNOW HOW TO TAKE A PROFIT.

60/40 = 20% Profit

No trader is going to make a profit 100% of the time. As such, the %'s used for LOSS and PROFIT are based on a 60/40 system. For every 10 trades: AVG. PROFIT of 20% on 6, and AVG. LOSS of 25% on 4 = gross of 20% (amount invested equal all 10 times). You only have to make a Profit on **60% OF THE TRADES** IF YOU LIMIT your LOSS on the other 40%.

You have a Fund of $1000, and each month you make 10 trades of $500 each: 6 gains @ 20% - 4 Losses @ 25% = +20% x $500 = +$100 (10% of Fund). With a return of 10% per month, the Fund doubles to $2K in 10 months. If the 10% is compounded, the Fund doubles in approx. 7.2 mos. In approx. 7.2 mos. more, the I.F. is now at $4000.

1 Week of Trades Using $ Management:

DATE	STK SYM	STK PRICE	BUY/SELL	OPTION	EXPIRE	PRICE	# CTRCTS	AP/AR INCL FEE	TRADE+/-	INV.FUND $500	FUND +/-
Mon7/08	AAPL	416.2	BUY	PUT 400	JY/12th	$0.62	4	($261)			
Mon7/08		411.9	SELL			$1.27	4	$495	$234	$734	$234
Mon7/08	QCOM	60.6	BUY	PUT 60	JY/12th	$0.32	6	($207)			
Mon7/08		60	SELL			$0.53	6	$303	$96	$830	$330
Tue7/09	AAPL	413.2	BUY	CALL 430	JY/12th	$0.27	10	($278)			
Tue7/09		422.3	SELL			$1.18	10	$1,162	$884	$1,714	$1,214
Tue7/09	NFLX	241.4	BUY	CALL 250	JY/12th	$1.26	2	($264)			
Tue7/09		245.8	SELL			$2.66	2	$520	$256	$1,970	$1,470
Wed7/10	LNKD	191	BUY	CALL 195	JY/12th	$1.07	2	($226)			
Wed7/10		190.5	SELL			$0.82	2	$152	($74)	$1,896	$1,396
Wed7/10	LNKD	190.5	BUY	PUT 185	JY/12th	$0.62	5	($324)			
Wed7/10		187.7	SELL			$0.94	5	$456	$132	$2,028	$1,528
Wed7/10	AMZN	290.4	BUY	CALL 295	JY/12th	$0.80	4	($333)			
Wed7/10		292.2	SELL			$1.18	4	$459	$126	$2,154	$1,654
Fri7/12	LNKD	197.2	BUY	CALL 200	JY/12th	$0.45	5	($239)			
Fri7/12		200	SELL			$0.95	5	$461	$221	$2,375	$1,875
Fri7/12	NFLX	251	BUY	CALL 255	JY/12th	$0.50	5	($264)			
Fri7/12		253.2	SELL			$1.10	5	$536	$272	$2,647	$2,147

1 WEEK   9 TRADES RISK HIGH:$333   RISK LOW:$207   8 GAINS 1 LOSS   TTL:+$2147

NOTE: In the 1 week worksheet of trades (see Chapter #1) there were 9 trades with a total Risk of $2346, which averaged a Risk of $260 each trade. The 8 Gains had an average Return of $268; with a low Return of $96 on $207 Risk for a 46% Profit, and a High Return of $884 on a $278 Risk for a 317% Profit. If we eliminate the high and low, we had 6 gains on a Risk of $1167 with a Return of $194 for an average 62% Profit. Obviously, averaging a 20% profit on trades is more than reasonable if you use the OC trading strategy.

CHAPTER #10

WHICH OPTION TO BUY?

You're looking at a chart of a stock from your watch list, and there is a Buy signal. You look at the stock options chain and now face the big question, Which Option To Buy? We are going to match Charts with Chains to answer the big question. Notice the TIME of the charts & chains because we are going to use actual TIME ELAPSE sequences for some of the examples. Because there are many examples, this Course Part will be broken into segments.

NOTE: all the Buys stay within a starting Investment Fund of $1000.

Chart #1: LNKD BUY SIGNAL

Chart #1: Notice the market open, 09:30 is @ (1). The chart carries over from the previous session so both the 5MA and 20MA will have enough frames to give us an accurate average. The first Green has a long Upper Shadow showing Resistance at the Upper Price Channel. The 2nd Green, (2), pushes through the Price Channel, but is still showing a big Upper Shadow.

The BUY is strong: 3rd gain since Open; no upper shadow; price channel still moving up; it is after a cross-over and there is now separation between the

MA's; it is above the last 3 points of Resistance, (R), from the previous session.

Chart #1:

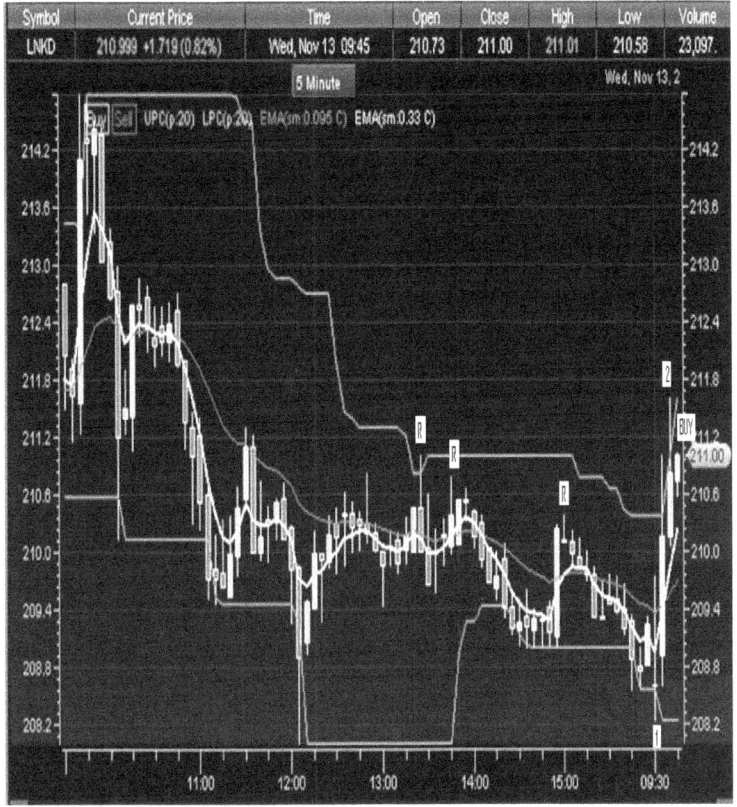

CHAIN #1 LNKD BUY CALL

We have a strong BUY CALL indicator, and Chain #1 lists the options. Notice the same stock price (1) as the Chart. Our Fund is $500, (we split the $1k into 2 parts), which strike price do we buy?

Chain #1:

| Symbol: LNKD | Last 210.999 | +1.719 (+0.82%) | Bid 210.85 x 400 | Ask 210.99 x 100 | Vol 22... |

| Chain Calls & Puts | Strikes 11 | Near 210.925 | Contract Type Standard |

Nov 16 '13 | Nov 22 '13 | Nov 29 '13 | Dec 6 '13 | Dec 21 '13 | Jan 18 '14 | Feb 22 '14

STANDARD OPTIONS (100 shares per contract)

Calls >   Nov 16 '13   < Puts

Open In.	Tot. Vol.	$ Chg.	Last Tr.	Bid	Ask	Strike P.	Bid	Ask	Last Tr.	$ Chg.	Tot. Vol.	Open In.
519	0	0.00	27.40	24.65	26.65	185.00	0.03	0.09	0.07	0.00	0	1022
654	0	0.00	20.50	19.85	21.65	190.00	0.07	0.11	0.10	0.00	25	891
304	0	0.00	15.20	14.80	16.60	195.00	0.16	0.18	0.17	-0.04	59	1580
522	1	+0.10	9.50	11.00	11.50	200.00	0.36	0.40	0.38	-0.15	1,029	3401
1506	22	+1.00	6.80	6.70 S1	7.10	205.00	0.93	0.99	1.00	-0.51	455	3387
1332	110	+0.73	3.45	3.30 S2 B1	3.55	210.00	2.39	2.54	2.41	-1.19	132	2566
2125	311	+0.28	1.33	1.29 S3 B2	1.39	215.00	5.30	5.50	5.52	-1.33	73	2224
2831	116	+0.06	0.40	0.39 B3	0.43	220.00	9.25	9.80	9.50	-1.87	14	1968
3038	51	+0.01	0.13	0.11	0.14	225.00	13.75	14.50	14.01	-1.99	23	1713

USE MARKET ORDERS

First, we work off of the Ask for the BUY because we enter Market orders, not Limit Orders. While trying to Buy for less than the Ask might save a few pennies now and then, if the Buy Indicator was strong, the stock price, and option price should continue to go up as you wait for the Ask to go down and meet your Limit Order.

REMEMBER: the strategy is for Quick Strike trades and profits!

QUICK PROFIT ESTIMATE

Using Chain #1 Above

The simplest way to calculate the best strike price is as follows: subtract the Ask premium from the Bid of the next higher strike price (deeper ITM, or closer to ITM) which will equal a quick profit estimate (QPE) of return per contract; then multiply by the number of contracts you can Buy at the Ask.

For example: Subtract the 210 S.P. ASK of 3.55 (B1), from the 205 BID of 6.70 (S1) = 315: 315 is the estimated gain if the stock gains 1 strike price, in this instance, $5. Now multiply the 315 by the # of contracts you can buy @ $3.55 (x 100 = $355), in this case 1, and your gain estimate for CALL-210 is $315.

CALL-215 Ask is $1.39 (B2), subtracted from CALL-210 Bid at $3.30 (S2) ='s $1.91. Now multiply $191 by # of contracts you can buy @ Ask $1.39: (x100 = 139) x 3 (500 divided by 139) ='s $573 est. gain. {(S2) 3.30 – 1.39 (B2) = 1.91 x 3 = $573}.

At this point, Buying 3 CALL-215 contracts @ $139 each, has better profit potential than Buying 1 CALL-210 contract @ $355.

CALL-220 Ask is $0.43 (B3), subtracted from CALL-215 Bid @ $1.29 (S3) ='s $0.86. Now multiply $86 x 10 (# of contracts): ='s $860 est. gain.

The best estimated profit potential is to Buy CALL-220 @ $.43 for a risk of $430.

Chain #2: SELL @ 10:12:

Open In.	Tot Vol.	$ Chg.	Last Tr.	Bid	Ask	Strike P.	Bid	Ask	Last Tr.	$ Chg.	Tot. Vol.	Open In.
654	0	0.00	20.50	23.15	25.50	190.00	0.05	0.08	0.05	-0.05	41	891
304	0	0.00	15.20	18.15	20.45	195.00	0.06	0.09	0.08	-0.13	155	1580
522	1	+0.10	9.50	13.45	14.90	200.00	0.17	0.21	0.17	-0.36	1,237	3401
1506	60	+3.90	9.70	9.30	9.80	205.00	0.54	0.60	0.55	-0.96	949	3387
1332	403	+2.93	5.65	5.50	5.75	210.00	1.54	1.63	1.58	-2.02	701	2566
2125	1,427	+1.76	2.81	2.69	2.75	215.00	3.55	3.80	3.65	-3.20	991	2224
2831	381	+0.66	1.00	$1.00	1.08	220.00	6.75	7.55	6.61	-4.76	38	1968
3038	246	+0.23	0.35	0.30	0.35	225.00	10.80	11.60	11.10	-4.90	172	1713

RESULTS: the Sell was made at 10:12 (1), approx. a 27 Minute trade with a stock price gain of $3: CALL-220 Buy at $0.43 x 10 contracts: Risk $448 (includes fees). Sell at $1.00 x 10 = Return $982 (-fees): PROFIT +$544 (+121%).

If Buy Call-215: Buy @ $1.39 x 3 = Risk $430. Sell @ $2.69 x 3 = Rtn $794 = PROFIT +$364 (85%).

If Buy Call-210: Buy @ $3.55 x 1 = Risk $366. Sell @ $550 x 1 = Rtn $539 = PROFIT $173 (47%).

Obviously, the CALL-220 made more profit because of the increased number of contracts bought. If you compare contracts 1:1, then the CALL-210 is the best Risk. Usually, if you can only afford to buy 1 contract, you want to Buy ITM, or as close to being ITM as possible.

Using CHART #1

Another crucial factor is NOT to buy too far OTM. If you look at Chart #1 (pg. 32) again, the day before session had a range of $6. Thus, it was not unreasonable to target a range of $2 more from point of buy. If the price had only moved to $213, instead of $214, it was still enough to make a profit on the CALL-220 because there was still almost 3 sessions before expiration. Also note there was already over 100 contracts traded in the first 15 minutes of trading.

NOTE: there is an OC TOOL to use for easy calculation of the QPE returns.

CHAPTER #10 Part #2

WHICH OPTION TO BUY?

Chart #2:

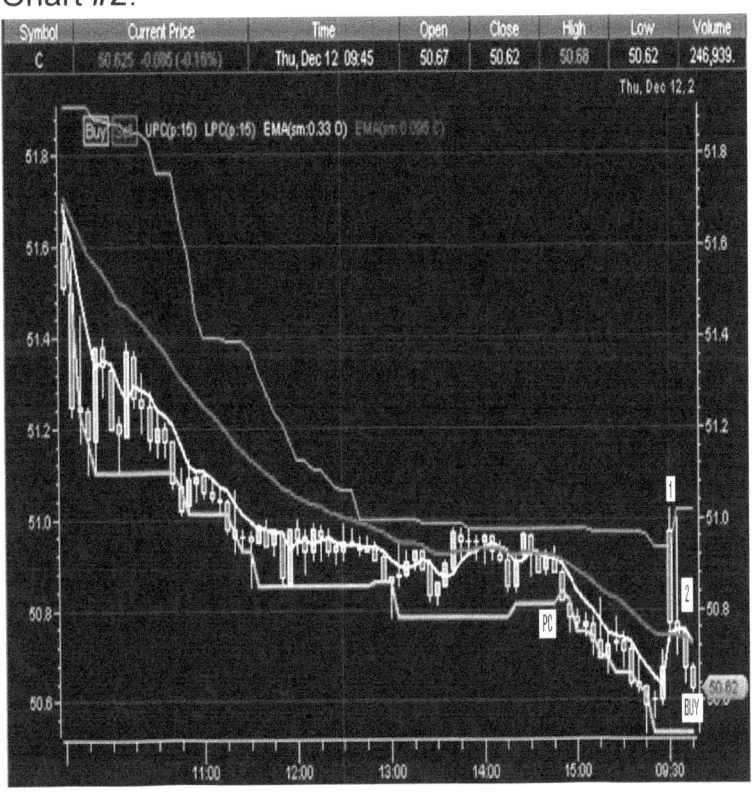

Chart #2 shows a strong Buy indicator: stock opens higher (1) than it closed day before, but drops all the way back to the previous 20MA, which is also now the new 5MA. It makes another run up, but fails creating a long Upper Shadow, and pushes under the 5MA, and the previous long Price Channel (PC). At (2) the entire body is now under both MA's. The question is whether there is enough room for the stock to drop and make a Put Profit because the levels are only $0.20.

REMEMBER to always note the levels. The drop at (1) looks impressive but is only a $0.20 drop, and there is only a $0.09 drop from the Buy to the Lower Price Channel. However, this is a $50 stock and even a $0.10 option gain can make a profit. First, take a quick look at the Daily Chart.

Chart #3: Daily

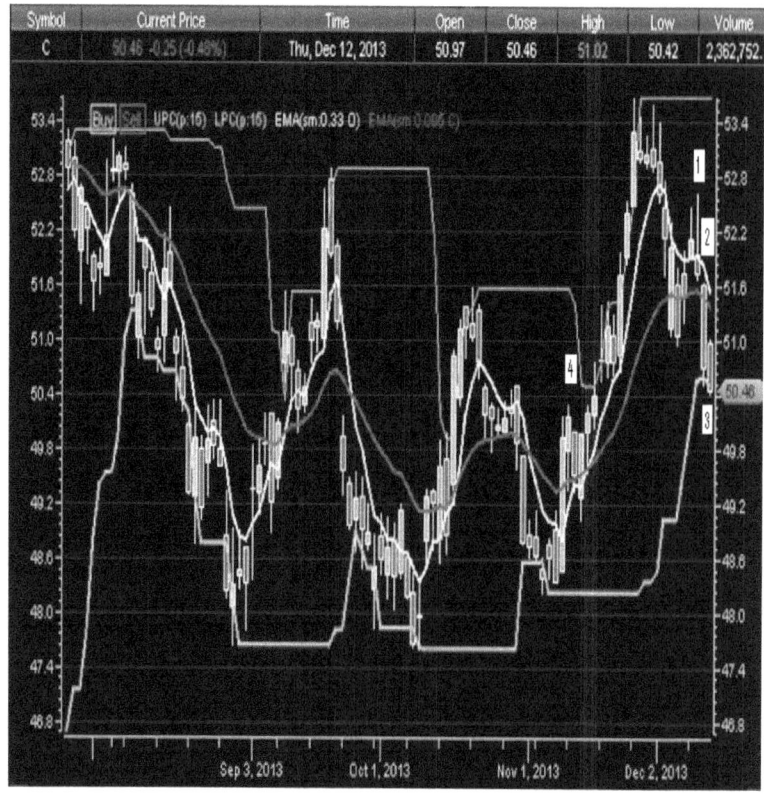

Use the Daily Chart as another indicator tool to support a Buy or Sell. In Chart #3, at (1), notice the long Upper Shadow, and the fact the body is now under the 5MA. At (2), the down trend continues crashing through the 20MA all the way to the Lower Price Channel at $50.49, which is also equal to a previous Upper Price Channel at (4). When the stock Opens at $50.97, (3), and starts to drop, this is a strong indicator it might drop $.50+ to the low of yesterday, which is enough room for a Put Buy even though the 5MA has not crossed the 20MA. Note the Chart levels here are $0.60.

Chain #3: C BUY-PUT:

Chain #3: Note the same stock price as the 5Min. Chart:

Symbol	C		Last	50.625		-0.085 (-0.17%)	Bid	50.62 x 1900	Ask	50.63 x 1900	Vol
Chain	Calls & Puts		Strikes	11	Near	50.625		Contract Type	Standard		

| Dec 13 '13 | Dec 21 '13 | Dec 27 '13 | Jan 3 '14 | Jan 10 '14 | Jan 18 '14 | Feb 22 '14 |

STANDARD OPTIONS (100 shares per contract)

Dec 13 '13

Calls >								< Puts			
Open In.	Tot. Vol.	$ Chg.	Last Tr.	Bid	Ask	Strike P.	Bid	Ask	Last Tra.	$ Chg.	Tot. Vol.	Open In.
52	0	0.00	5.05	2.61	2.71	48.00	0.00	0.02	0.24	+0.23	20	160
0	0	n/a	0.00	2.11	2.36	48.50	0.00	0.01	0.01	0.00	0	313
330	0	0.00	3.10	1.62	1.72	49.00	0.00	0.05	0.02	0.00	0	1515
469	0	0.00	1.49	1.15	1.25	49.50	0.02	0.06	0.06	0.00	0	528
564	32	+0.04	0.84	0.73	0.82	50.00	0.11	0.13	0.09	-0.06	2	1071
1272	136	-0.06	0.41	0.40	0.43	50.50	0.26	0.29	0.27	-0.05	23	1159
5633	1,230	-0.02	0.20	0.18	0.20	51.00	0.53	0.58 BUY	0.56	+0.01	144	5437
3616	5	0.00	0.10	0.06	0.09	51.50	0.90	0.97	0.80	-0.19	436	3743
4320	206	-0.03	0.03	0.03	0.04	52.00	1.37	1.43	1.37	-0.06	11	1684

First, note the Strike Price levels are $.50 apart. Because the target is only about a $.20 move, Buy ITM when possible. Note the volume of 50.50 at only 23 (1), and 51.00 at 144. S.P. 51.00 also has the most Open Interest, and the only $ Chg. Gain (2) ITM.

Doing a QPE: Put-51 +.32 x 8 (Risk $482) = $256 vs. Put-51.50 +.40 x 5 (Risk 500) = $200. In this case, the estimates are based upon a $.50 (1 level) stock price drop (which for a Put is a gain).

CHART #4: C: 5 Min. after Buy (1):

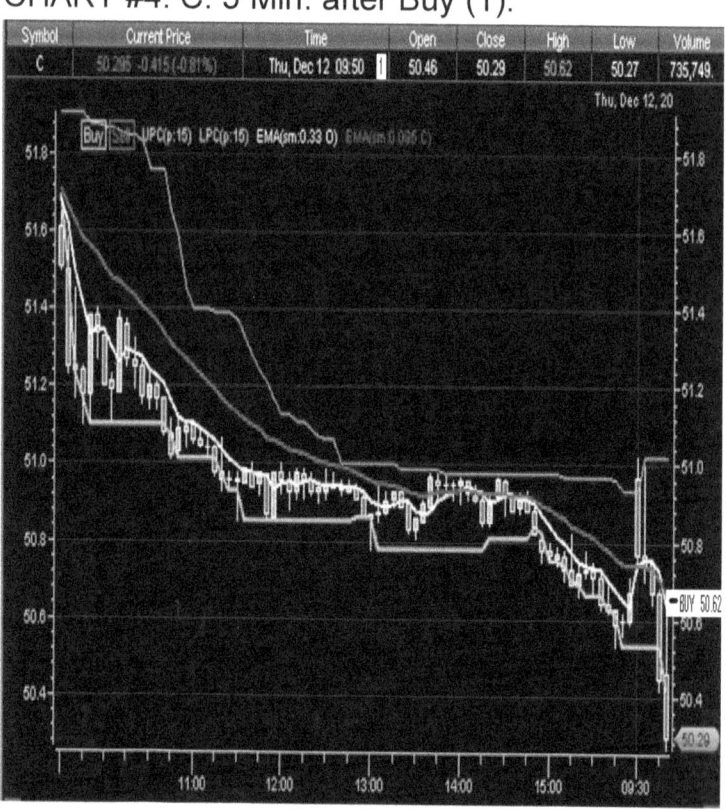

Notice time @ (1). This will give you an idea of watching a chart develop via real time elapse frames. No reason to Sell at this time: lower PC still being pushed down; upper shadow; 5MA crossing under 20MA. However, notice the range of session before: approx. .90. The range for today is already at .70 and bears close watching.

Chain #3: 5 Min. after Buy: Stock drop $.33 and Option +$.20.

Open In	Tot Vol	$ Chg	Last Tr	Bid	Ask	Strike P	Bid	Ask	Last Tra	$ Chg	Tot Vol	Open In
52	0	0.00	5.05	2.27	2.48	48.00	0.01	0.02	0.24	+0.23	20	160
0	0	n/a	0.00	1.76	2.02	48.50	0.00	0.02	0.01	0.00	50	313
330	0	0.00	3.10	1.29	1.44	49.00	0.00	0.05	0.02	0.00	0	1515
469	87	-0.59	0.90	0.86	0.91	49.50	0.08	0.10	0.07	+0.01	21	528
564	32	+0.04	0.84	0.48	0.52	50.00	0.20	0.23	0.22	+0.07	52	1071
1272	454	-0.21	0.26	0.23	0.26	50.50 +15	0.44	0.48	0.27	-0.05	23	1159
5633	1,871	-0.11	0.11	0.10	0.12	51.00 +20	0.78	0.84	0.67	+0.12	150	5437
3616	5	0.00	0.10	0.04	0.06	51.50 +20	1.17	1.24	1.24	+0.25	791	3743
4320	212	-0.03	0.03	0.02	0.04	52.00	1.44	1.77	1.37	-0.06	11	1684

Notice the volume on 50.50 is STILL 23 with the same "Last Trade". Even though the Bid equates to a +.15 over the Ask at the time of the Buy, no trades have been made. If a Market Sell Order is entered right now for the 51.00 position, it will sell immediately for the $0.78 Bid Price, which is +.20 on a .58 Buy (34%) x 8 which = a +$160 gross in 5 minutes. Even with a strong Chart, a Sell here would be reasonable.

Chart #5: C-SELL: 10 Min. after Buy:

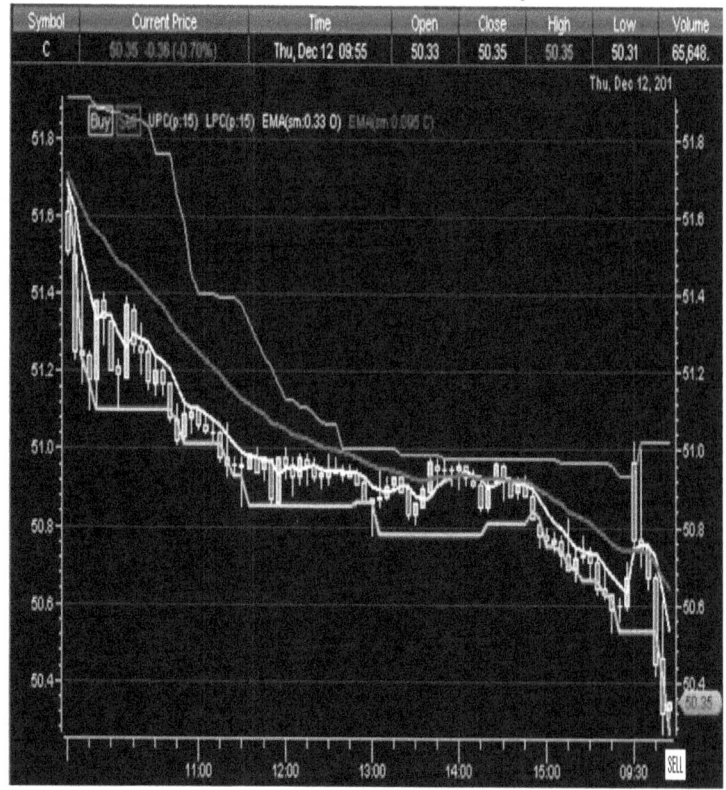

The Sell is good even though it is at the very first indication of reversal: the previous frame shows a Lower Shadow; the 50.35 represents a retraction of $.08 which is almost 25% of the move since the Buy; and the Bid @ $0.75 equals a profit of 21%.

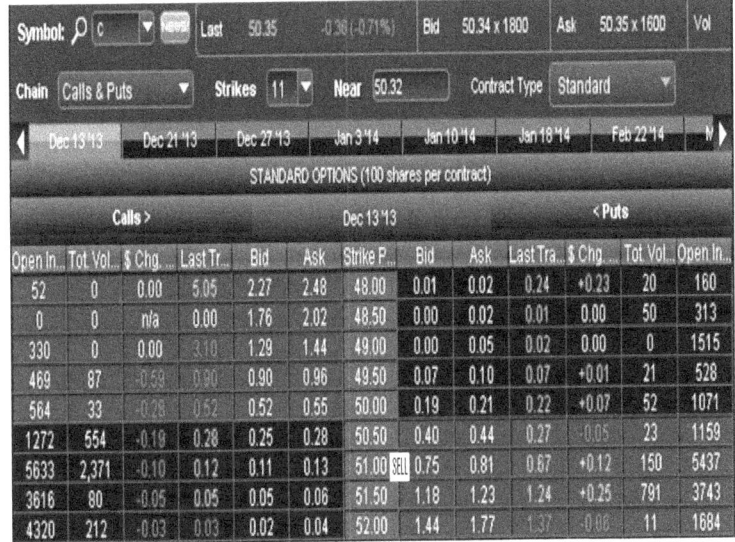

ADE RESULTS: Buy Put-51 at $.58 x 8 = $482 (Risk): Sell at $.75 x 8 = $582 (Return) = +$100 Profit = 21% net.

Results IF Buy 51.50 at $.97 x 5 = $500 (Risk): Sell @ $1.18 = $575 (Return) = +$75 Profit = 15% net.

Chart #6: 5 Min. for entire day:

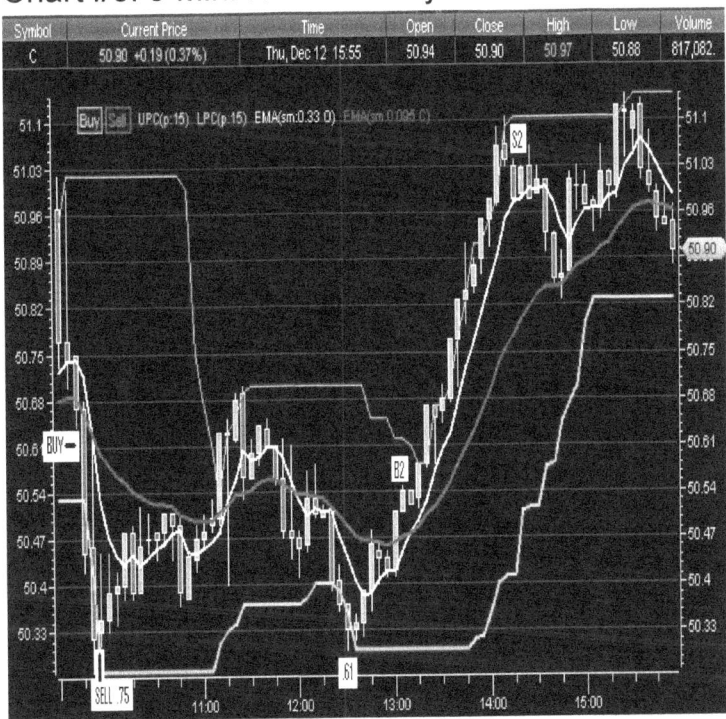

Looking at the entire 5 Min. Chart for the day, the Sell was excellent. Even though the stock price dropped back to $50.30 at 12:30 (.61), the option never traded for more than $0.61, $0.14 less than at the Sell. Note the great Buy-Call @ B2 & Sell @ S2. It is not unusual for one stock to offer both a Call & Put opportunity in the same session.

CHAPTER #10 Part #3

WHICH OPTION TO BUY?

Chart #7: AAPL Daily:

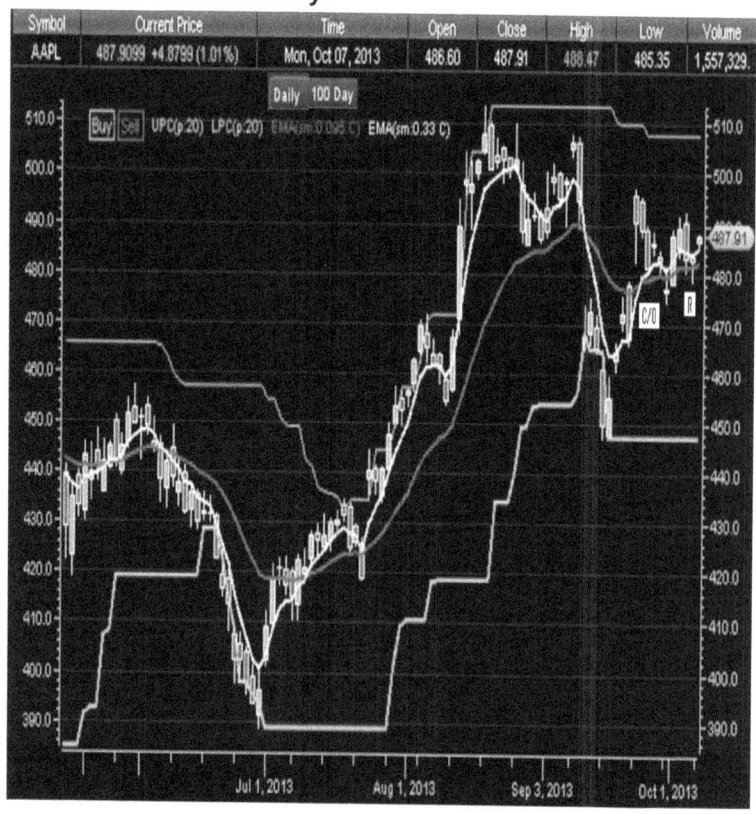

Chart #7, 100 Day, shows a strong indicator to Buy a Call: after the cross-over (C/O) the 5MA does not go under the 20MA; the session opens above the previous close and above the 5MA; there is resistance (R) to dropping on the two previous sessions. Now we go to the 5Min. Chart.

Chart #8: AAPL BUY:

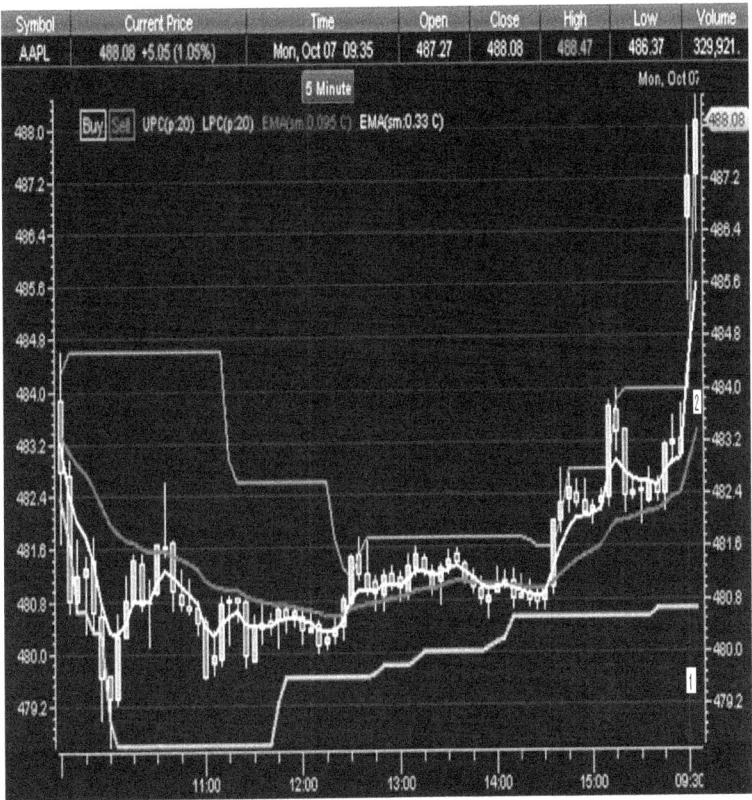

Note where the 09:30 open (1) actually starts. Even though there is only 2 time frames for the new session, Chart #8 indicates a very strong Buy Call: the Daily Chart supports a gain; the Open pushes through the Upper Price Channel; a big jump at the Open; the 1st frame is Green; the 2nd (2) frame opens higher than the 1st and closes Green; the 2nd frame has a bigger body than the 1st frame; both frames have longer lower shadows than upper shadows.

Chain #6: AAPL: BUY

Chain #6: AAPL: BUY

Open In.	Tot.Vol	$ Chg.	Last Tr.	Bid	Ask	Strike P.	Bid	Ask	Last Tr.	$ Chg.	Tot Vol.	Open In.
427	26	+4.27	23.50	23.35	23.70	465.00	0.43	0.46	0.44	-0.51	448	2959
1286	68	+3.65	19.00	18.65	19.10	470.00	0.81	0.85	0.82	-0.85	795	3786
1513	398	+3.14	14.59	14.50	14.80	475.00	1.50	1.56	1.55	-1.26	234	3092
3260	768	+2.80	10.80	10.65	10.90	480.00	2.66	2.74	2.70	-2.09	328	3395
4098	1,217	+2.25	7.55	7.40	7.60	485.00	4.40	4.50	4.42	-2.83	665	3063
5088	2,297	+1.51	4.86	4.85 ❶	4.95	490.00	6.75	6.95	6.85	-3.05	347	1734
5618	1,829	+0.96	2.95	2.99 ❸	3.00	495.00	9.80	10.05	10.05	-3.45	82	768
7689	1,681	+0.47	1.70	1.72 ❷	1.75	500.00	13.45	13.80	13.80	-3.65	25	1152

When deciding which Option to Buy, and you can only buy the same amount of contracts at different Strike Prices (1,1), and both are OTM, usually pick the one closest to ITM: in this case, SP-490 vs. SP-495. Before you go any further, do a QPE Return on the three Strike Prices numbered using the formula (Bid minus Ask) we used before, and decide which Option Strike Price you would buy using a $510 budget. Don't figure fees in your quick estimate.

The Quick Profit Estimate on the three Strike Prices are:

SP-490 = $245 (7.40 – 4.95 = 2.45 x 1).

SP-495 = $185 (4.85-3.00 = 1.85 x 1).

SP-500 = $248 (2.99 – 1.75 = 1.24 x 2).

Since both SP-490 & SP-500 show equal Profit Potential, and SP-490 is much closer to ITM, usually, the best Call Option to buy would be SP-

490. However, SP-500 cost a lot less, thus, has a much better % of return potential. Now let's look at the Chain below, #7, and see how the Options did.

Chart #9: AAPL: 20 Min. after Buy:

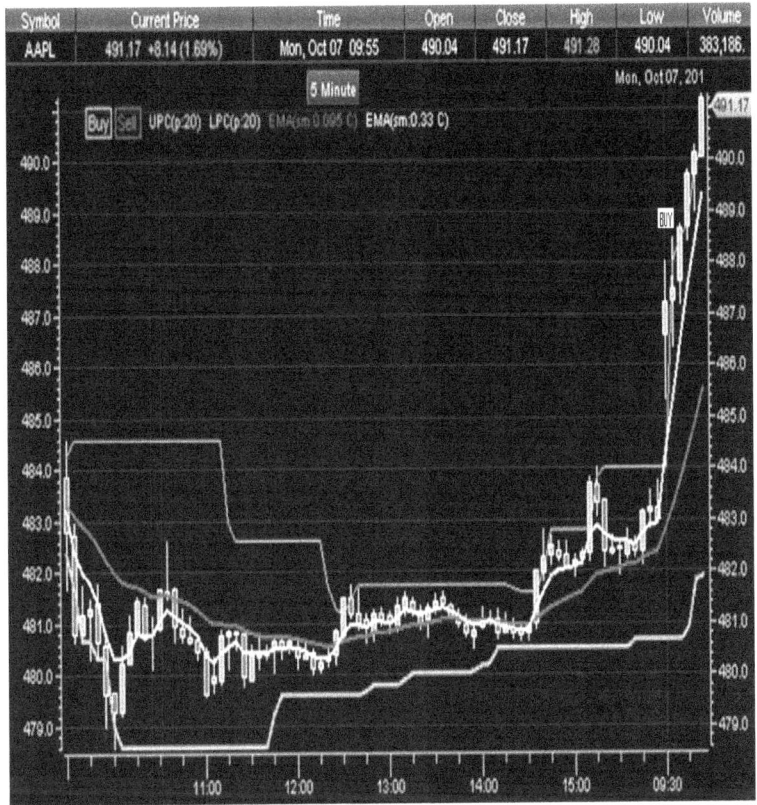

The Chart above, #9, 20 minutes later, shows the Buy Point was excellent. No Sell signal. However, if you go back to the Daily Chart, #7, notice the previous Resistance at $490 since the C/O. The amount of profit combined with the Resistance makes a good Sell right now.

CHAIN #7: AAPL:

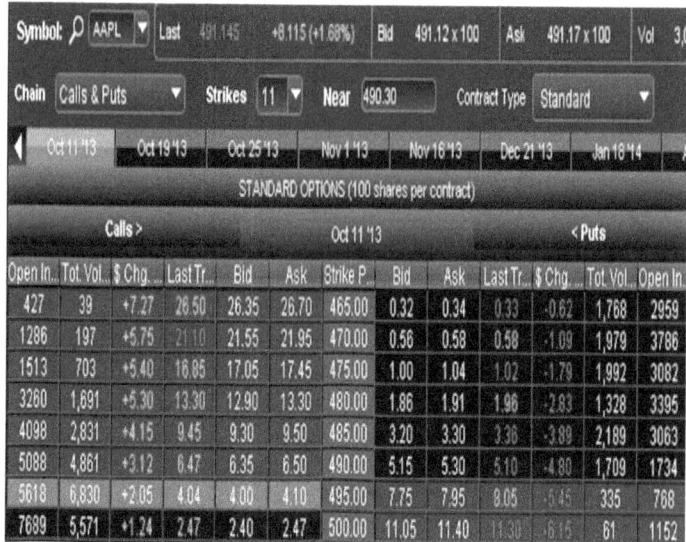

SP-490: BUY @ $495, SELL @ $635 = +$140 (+28%).

SP-495: BUY @ $300, SELL @ $400 = +$100 (+33%).

SP-500: BUY @ $350, SELL @ $480 = +$130 (37%) (Buy 2 contracts).

Even though SP-490 had the lowest Return % of the 3 Options, it had the Highest $ amount of profit. The QPE is pretty accurate for a Quick Estimate.

Chart #10: AAPL:

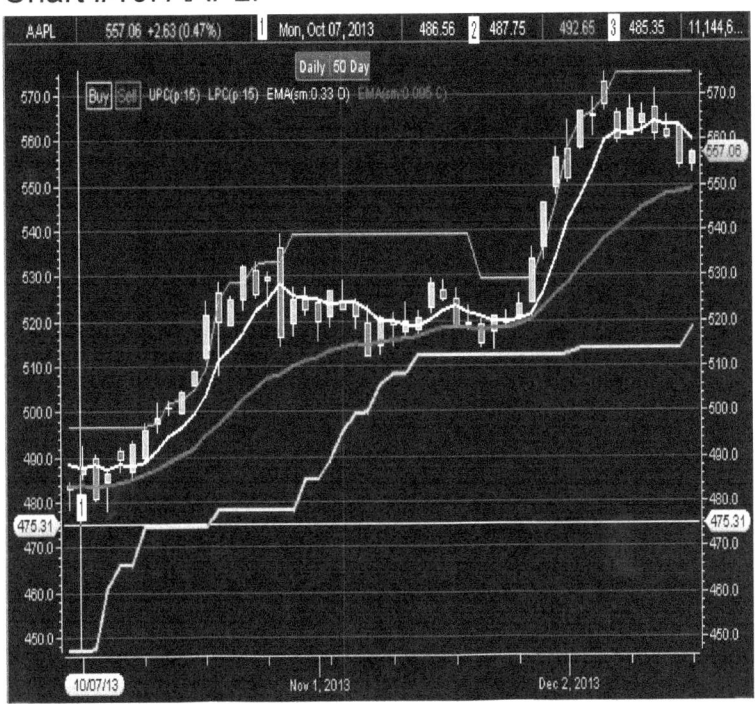

The Daily Chart above, #10, shows the current price (557.06) for 12/16. However, Oct. 07 (1), is highlighted by the crosshair (1), showing the open & close (2), and the high-low range (3). Notice the high for the day is 492.65. If you had kept AAPL longer, sometime during the session it would have gained another 1.48 more than Chart #9. However, also note the day closed @ 487.75, which is 3.42 less than Chart #9; and .33 less than at the time of the Buy. KEY TO SUCCESS: TAKE A PROFIT

CHAPTER #10 Part #4:

WHICH OPTION TO BUY?

In this part, we are going to follow an actual trade as time lapse frozen in 7 Charts, and 6 Chains. The first Chart, #11, is the 100 day chart up through the session before the trade. The following 6 5Min.

Charts & Chains will show time sequences from the time of Buy, to the time of Sell. Note the time of each chart is approx. 10 min. apart, except the last Chart, point of Sell, which is 5min after the one before it.

Before each Option Market Open, look at the Daily Charts for your Watch List stocks and make a note of the few which have good buy indicators. However, do not trade based upon the Daily Chart alone.

Chart #11: AAPL 100 DAY:

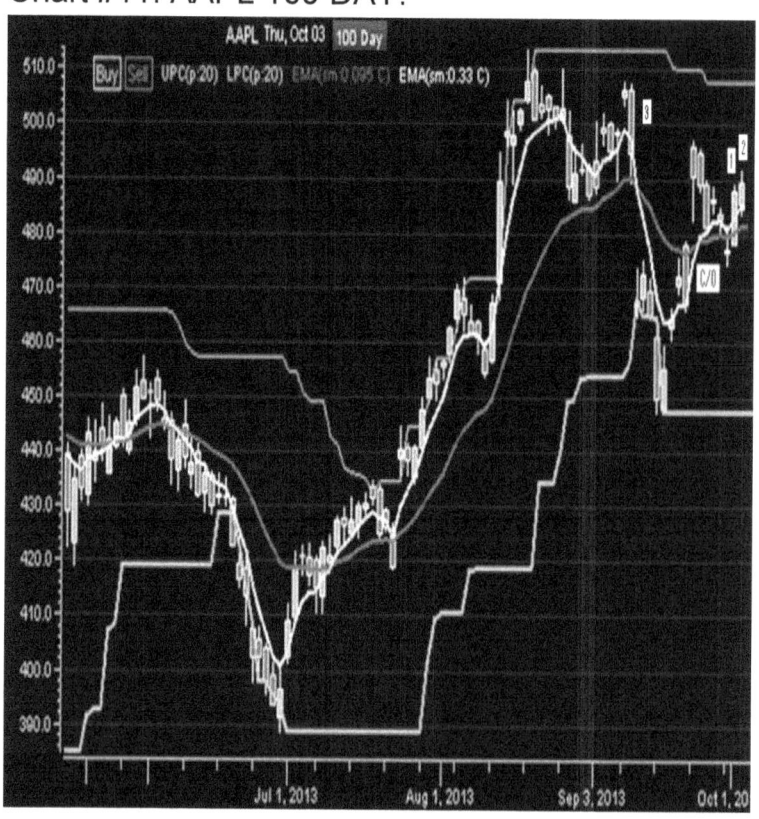

Chart #11, a Daily, shows a good Buy Call indicator for the next day: last two sessions had gains, (1-Tue.,2-Wed.); the 5MA bounced off the 20MA and now has separation; there is room for further gain to the next level, (3), where the 5MA started the last big move down resulting in a cross of the 20MA.

Chart #12: AAPL: BUY 5Min.

Chart #12, below, shows why it is always a good idea NOT to trade using just the Daily Chart. The 1st frame opens higher than the previous close, pushing through the Upper Price Channel. However, it then drops all the way down through the 5MA, to the 20MA and even with the close of the day before. The next couple of frames turn what looked like a strong Buy Call on the Daily Chart into a strong Buy Put on the 5Min. Chart.

BOUGHT ANALYSIS: All MKTS are Down; 2nd drop in a row; 5MA cross under 20MA; push thru bottom Price Channel. Note the time of 09:50.

Chart #12: AAPL 5Min. w/Buy:

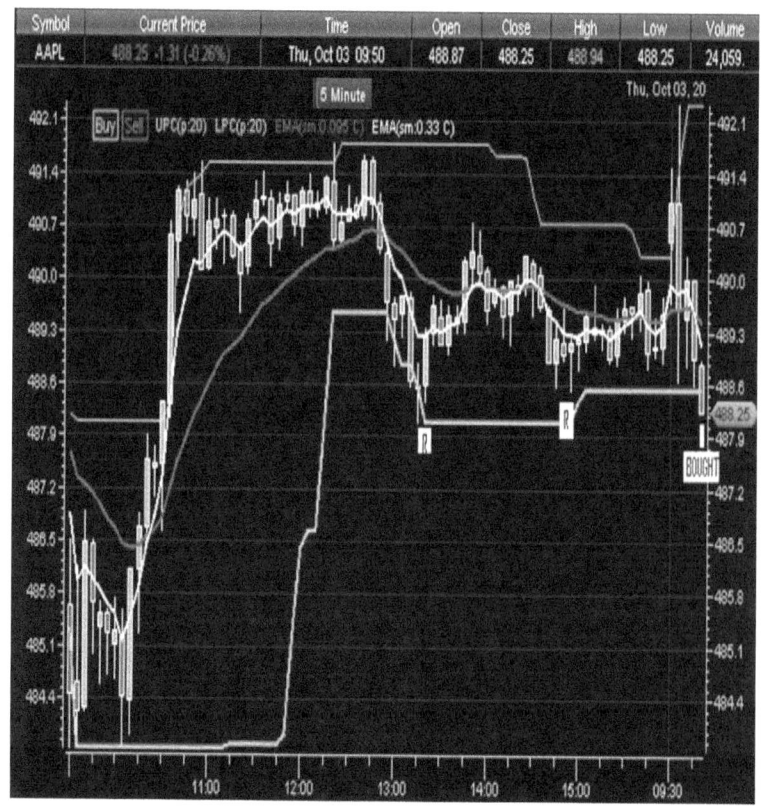

Chain #8: AAPL Buy Put

Look at the Chain, #8, to decide which SP to buy and consider these important factors: 1 day until expiration; the Chart price levels are at .70; the previous Resistance is just below current frame close; the upward Cross from yesterday at 486 could be a possible Resistance level today.

A QPE for 1, 2, and 3 (a fund of $500) shows: 1. +$3402. +434 3. +707. Obviously, #3 has the best Profit Potential, with excellent volume.

MARKET ORDER TRADE EXECUTED: BUY OCT. 4 PUT SP-480 @ $0.61 x 7.

Risk: $444. REMEMBER: you must have enough cash to cover Premium Price & fees. (For this course we set fees @ $10 a trade, and $1 per contract for easy calculation. Some brokers will have higher/lower trade or contract fees).

Chain #8: AAPL Buy Put:

Open In.	Tot. Vol.	$ Chg.	Last Tr.	Bid	Ask	Strike P.	Bid	Ask	Last Tr.	$ Chg.	Tot Vol.	Open In.
679	38	-0.04	24.35	23.15	23.65	465.00	0.06	0.07	0.07	0.00	46	4827
1052	30	-0.52	19.34	18.25	18.70	470.00	0.10	0.11	0.10	-0.03	320	7532
2083	115	-0.65	14.10	13.35	13.80	475.00	0.21	0.23	0.21	-0.07	605	7143
4600	365	-0.85	9.10	8.75	9.15	480.00	0.58	0.61	0.55	-0.08	1,367	8004
6152	1,440	-0.95	5.00	5.00	5.15	485.00	1.65	1.73	1.70	+0.18	1,992	5458
9871	4,993	-0.71	2.29	2.27	2.35	490.00	3.90	4.00	3.90	+0.40	2,653	4361
11987	3,692	-0.39	0.87	0.85	0.89	495.00	7.40	7.70	7.53	+0.93	680	2347

Chart #13 APPL @ 10:00

Chart #13: In 10 minutes the stock has dropped another .85 since the Buy (B),; the 5MA has increased the separation from the 20MA; each new frame Open has been equal to the previous Close; even though a new Lower Price Channel has started to form, the price has already pushed through it. No reason to Sell.

Chart#13: AAPL @ 10:00:

Chain #9: AAPL @ 10:00:

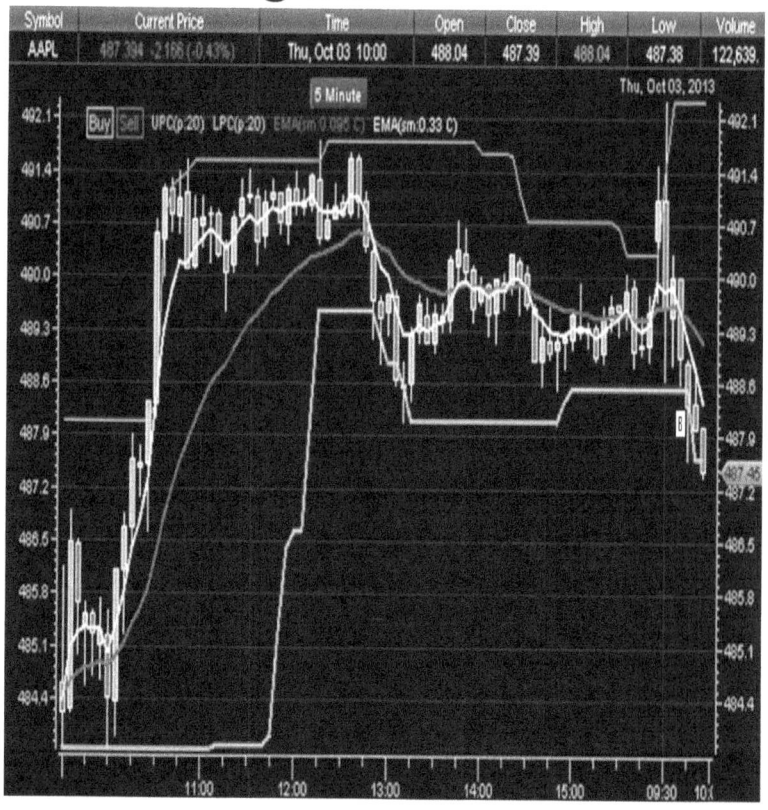

Option has gained .09, which is +$63. After fees profit is +$19, or 3.8% gain.

Chart #14: AAPL: 10:10

Chart #14: AAPL @ 10:10:

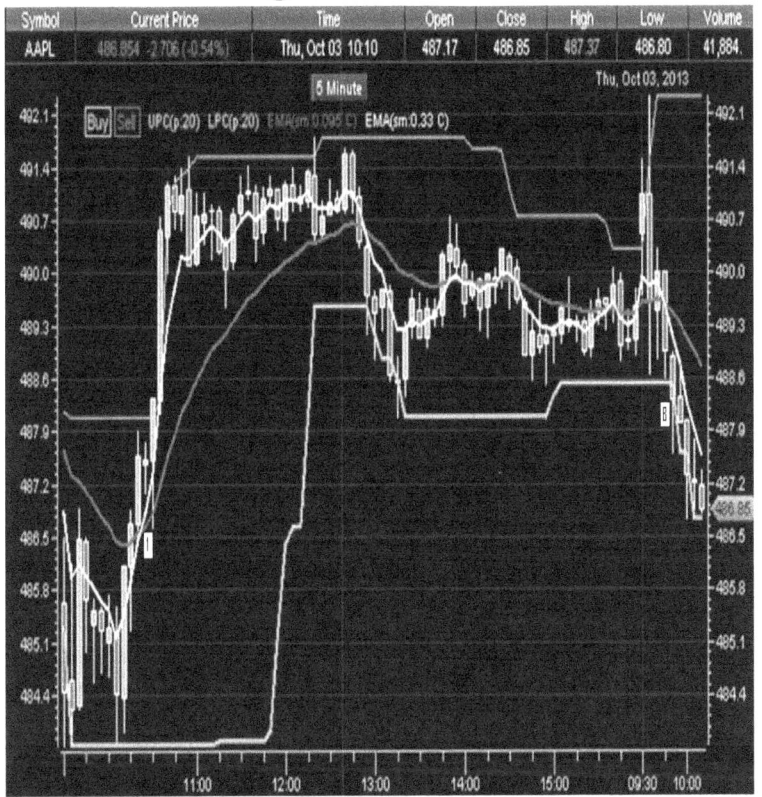

Chart #14: In 10 minutes the stock has dropped .60; the 5MA has increased the separation from the 20MA; some concern about the last 3 frames finding Resistance at the newly formed Lower Price Channel, which is about the same level as the cross @ 1.

Chain #10: AAPL @ 10:10:

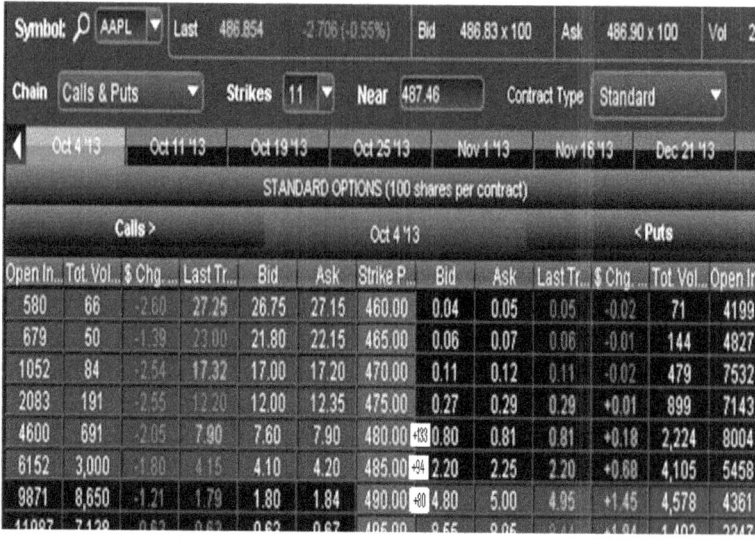

Note the Profits marked for each Strike Price from time of Buy. Right now the profit of $133 would be a net of +$99, which is a 22% gain on the $444 Risk. Since the Chart is still indicating a Put Trend, there is no reason to Sell right now.

Rather, a Trailing Stop of .10 is placed to ensure a Profit (see $ Management). This means, there is a Stop Loss Order at .70, (SP-480) which is .10 beneath the Bid. If the Bid goes up, the Stop Loss Order will also move up to stay within .10 of the Bid. However, if the Bid goes down, the Stop Loss Order DOES NOT go down. If the Bid goes down to the last Stop Order, say .70 right now, the Stop Loss Order triggers an immediate MARKET SELL ORDER. REMEMBER, the Stop Loss can be changed to a Market Sell at any time.

If Sold at .70, there is a gross profit of .09, which is +$63. The key is not to turn a profit into a loss.

Chart #15: AAPL @ 10:20:

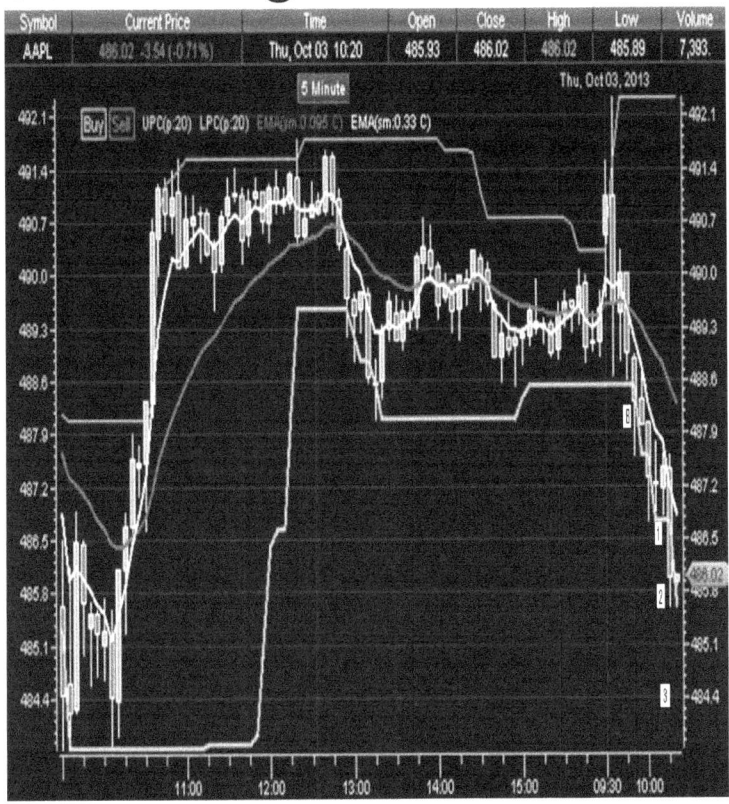

A drop of .92 since Chart #14. No Sell at the Green (1) because it did not push through the 5MA, and the Option only dropped about .04. No reason to Sell here: small Green body; Lower Price Channel still being pushed down; room to drop to (3).

Chain #11: AAPL @ 10:20:

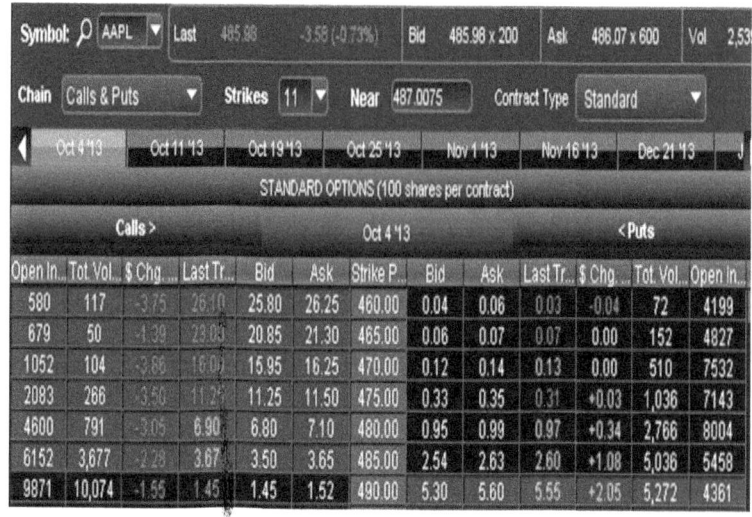

Notice the difference in the stock price between Chain #11 and Chart #15: In the time it took to copy the Chart, then the Chain (during streaming data), the price moved down another .04 which is good. The Option has gained another .15 (+105 net). Increased the Trailing Stop to .15 and is now at .80 (-.15 from Bid).

CHART #16: AAPL @ 10:25:

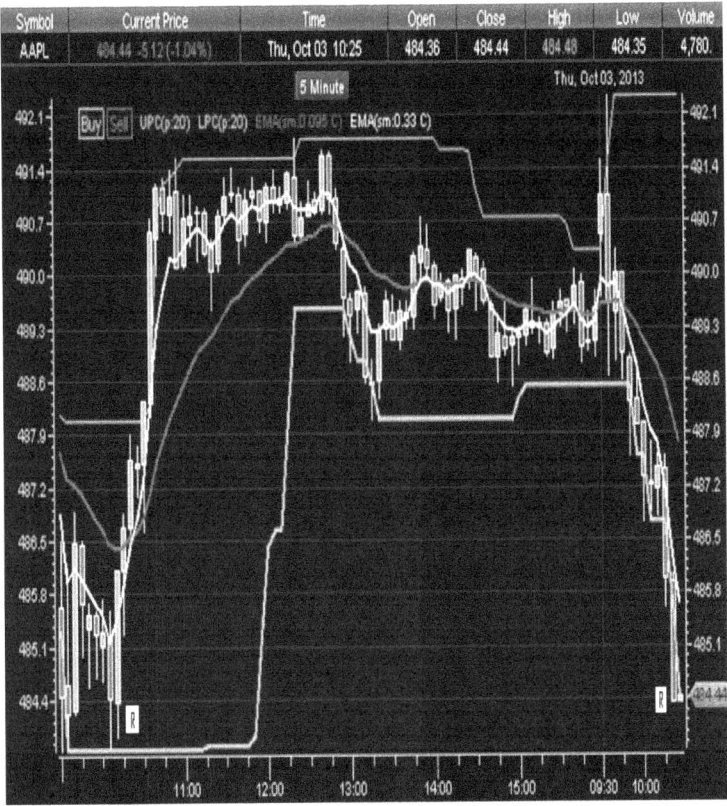

This is 5 Min. after the last Chart because of the 2 big drops in a row, and more importantly, this newly forming Green is at the level (R,R) of the start of the big gain from yesterday. The new Green is at the start of the next 5Min frame. Notice on the 100 Day Chart (beginning of this Seg.), today's drop is now equal to the 5MA, just above the 20MA, and may prove to be Resistance.

CHAIN #12: AAPL @ 10:25:

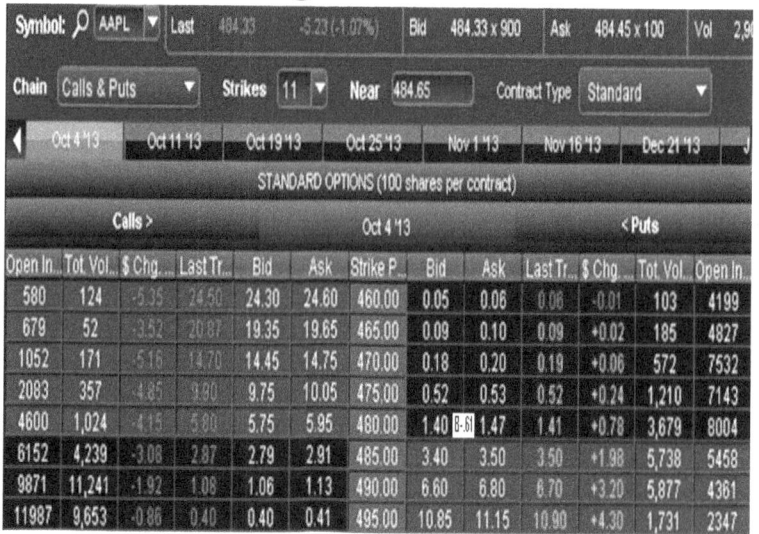

The Option had a gain of .45 in 5 minutes, and the profit is now +519 net.

CHART #17: AAPL @ 10:30 SELL:

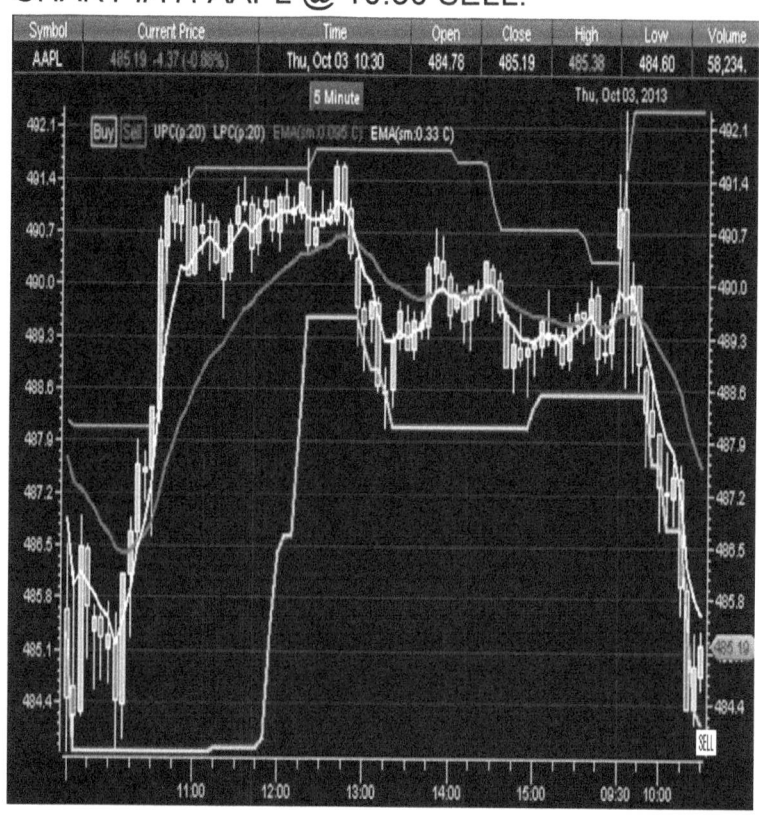

Definite SELL: 2nd Green in a row with a price gain of close to $1; Option price dropped quick (see Chain #13 next) which triggered Trailing Stop conversion to Market Sell. Even though the lower PC is still headed down, because of the previous Resistance at the same price, and the amount of profit, this SELL is late.

CHAIN #13: AAPL @ 10:30 SELL:

Symbol	AAPL	Last 485.19	-4.37 (-0.89%)		Bid 485.07 x 500		Ask 485.24 x 100		Vol 3,15
Chain	Calls & Puts		Strikes 11	Near 484.65		Contract Type	Standard		

| Oct 4 '13 | Oct 11 '13 | Oct 19 '13 | Oct 25 '13 | Nov 1 '13 | Nov 16 '13 | Dec 21 '13 |

STANDARD OPTIONS (100 shares per contract)

Oct 4 '13

Calls >							< Puts			
Open In.	Tot. Vol.	$ Chg.	Last Tr.	Bid	Ask	Strike P.	Bid	Ask	Last Tr.	$ Chg.	Tot. Vol.	Open In.
580	128	-5.11	24.74	25.00	25.45	460.00	0.05	0.07	0.05	-0.02	110	4199
679	52	-3.52	20.87	20.10	20.45	465.00	0.07	0.09	0.09	+0.02	199	4827
1052	207	-4.67	15.19	15.15	15.55	470.00	0.14	0.15	0.15	+0.02	617	7532
2083	406	-4.55	10.20	10.55	10.80	475.00	0.38	0.41	0.39	+0.11	1,553	7143
4600	1,186	-3.51	6.44	6.25	6.55	480.00	1.12 8-61 1.19		1.13	+0.50	5,089	8004
6152	6,490	-2.75	3.20	3.15	3.30	485.00	2.95 1.73 3.05		2.95	+1.43	6,605	5458
9871	12,177	-1.82	1.18	1.23	1.29	490.00	5.95 +1.00 6.25		6.25	+2.75	6,077	4361

TRADE RESULTS: BUY Put-480 @ .61 x 7 = Risk $444: SELL @ 1.12 = Return $767: PROFIT = +$323 (73%).

It is hard to criticize a 73% profit. However, the profit was as high as $519, which means a drop of close to 40% of the profit before the Sell. On Chart #15 the possible Resistance at $484 was noted. As such, when the 1st Green continued to move up, and the Option Bid dropped from $1.40 to $1.30, it was time for an immediate Market Sell.

Here are the Trade results for SP-485 & SP-490 if bought instead of SP-480:

SP-485: BUY @ 1.73 x2 = Risk $357: SELL @ 2.95 = Rtn $579 = Profit +$232 (64%).

SP-490: BUY @ 4.00 x1 = Risk $411: SELL @ 5.95 = Rtn $584 = Profit +$173 (42%).

CHAPTER #10 Part #5

WHICH OPTION TO BUY?

The BUY point is the most important factor in successful trading; the SELL point is the 2nd most important; and of course buying the right Option would be the 3rd most important factor. However, the right Option is dependent upon the right Buy; and of course, if the Sell point is wrong, it can negate the other two factors. As such, we are going to look at a couple more Buy/Sell Chart & Chain combinations before moving on.

CHART #18: AAPL CALL BUY 10/18:

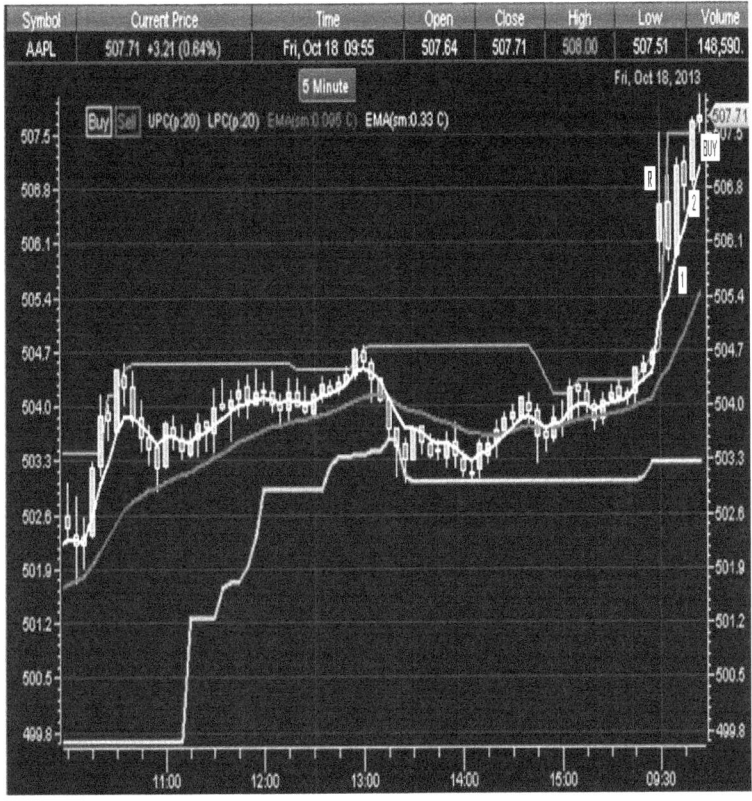

Chart #18 shows strong BUY CALL indicators: initial gain (R) at open; Green body at (1) stays above 5MA and goes above 1st frame close; Green body at (2) pushes through Upper Price Channel and overcomes 1st frame Shadow; increased separation between 5MA and 20MA; Buy is above previous frame close and is pushing PC up.

CHAIN #14: w/AAPL CHART #18:

Symbol: AAPL	Last 507.81	+3.31 (+0.66%)	Bid 507.73 x 200	Ask 507.86 x 300	Vol 2,36

Chain: Calls & Puts | Strikes: 11 | Near: 507.90 | Contract Type: Standard

Oct 19 '13 | Oct 25 '13 | Nov 1 '13 | Nov 8 '13 | Nov 16 '13 | Nov 22 '13 | Dec 21 '13

STANDARD OPTIONS (100 shares per contract)

Oct 19 '13

		Calls >							< Puts		
Open In.	Tot. Vol.	$ Chg.	Last Tr.	Bid	Ask	Strike P.	Bid	Ask	Last Tr.	$ Chg.	Tot. Vol.	Open In.
5757	622	+3.32	22.67	22.70	22.90	485.00	0.02	0.03	0.02	0.00	657	10127
12203	635	+3.38	17.88	17.65	17.90	490.00	0.03	0.04	0.03	0.00	674	12865
10318	1,515	+3.15	12.75	12.75	12.90	495.00	0.03	0.05	0.03	-0.06	2,294	8507
34321	4,993	+2.85	7.85	7.80	7.90	500.00	0.06	0.09	0.07	-0.41	4,244	21833
16626	7,241	+1.62	3.37	3.30	3.40	505.00	0.53	0.55	0.55	-1.74	7,671	6625
26654	10,354	+0.33	0.68	0.65	0.70	510.00	2.79	3.00	2.91	-2.99	1,325	9236
16469	2,954	-0.04	0.09	0.07	0.09	515.00	7.20	7.50	7.45	-3.30	75	1164
9957	755	-0.03	0.05	0.03	0.05	520.00	12.15	12.45	12.40	-3.25	114	2433

NOTE: Even though the Expiration date highlighted in blue says Oct. 19th, after close Friday the 18th, there is no more trading except to exercise or expire. As such, always Buy ITM, or as close as possible on last day of trading for the Option.

QPE: (1) SP-505 = Risk of $351 with Profit potential of +$469. (2) SP-510 = Risk of $436 with Profit potential of $1544. BUY SP-510 @ .70 x 6 = RISK $436.

CHART #19: AAPL 10/18 SELL:

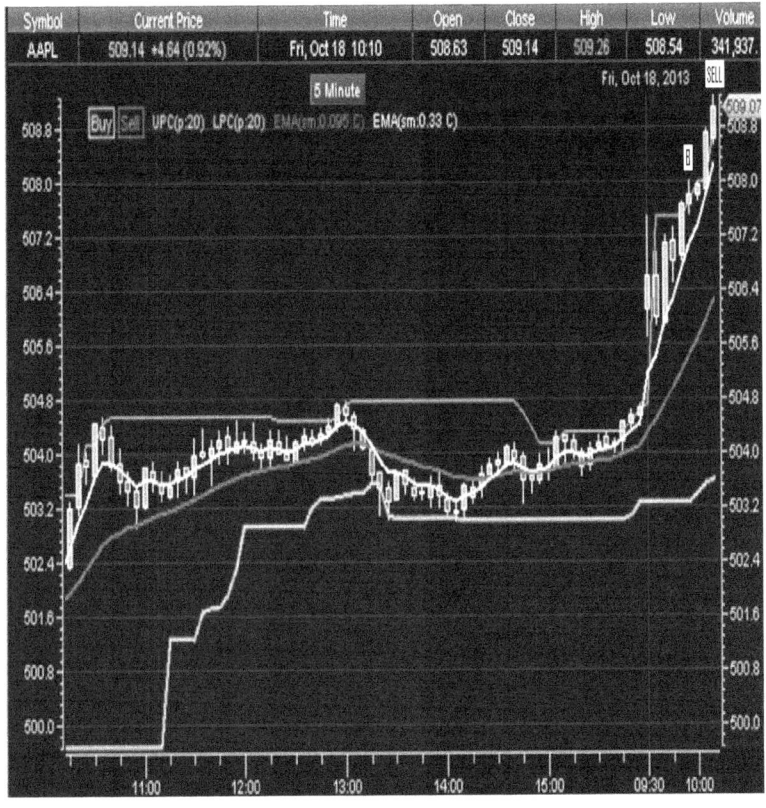

The point of Sell does NOT show a strong Sell indicator. The decision to Sell was based upon % of profit (see Chain #15 below); the Daily Chart; Option being OTM; the expected immediate Option price drop due to TV decrease if the stock reverses at all. For the day, AAPL had a High of 509.26, only .19 higher than time of sell.

CHAIN #15: w/AAPL CHART #19: SELL

TRADE Results:

SP-510 Buy @ 0.70 x 6 = Risk $436: Sell @ 1.06 = Rtn $620 = Profit +$184 (42%)

SP-505 Buy @ 3.40 x 1 = Risk $351: Sell @ 4.35 = Rtn $424 = Profit +$73 (20%).

Chart #20: Buy-Put @ 10:05

CHART #20:

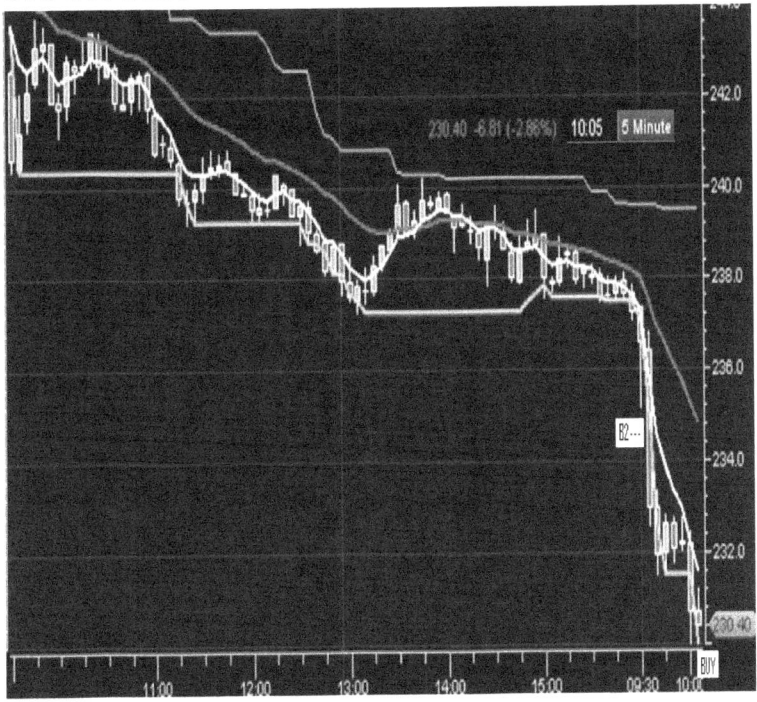

Chart #20 very good Buy indicator: 2nd Bottom Price Channel break through since open; under 5MA which has very good separation from 20MA. A better BUY was at the 2nd frame when the price dropped beneath the lower shadow of the 1st frame (B2).

CHAIN #16: w/CHART #20:

Calls >						Last 230.40	-6.81 (-2.87%)			< Puts			
Open In.	Tot. Vol.	$ Chg.	Last Tr.	Bid	Ask	Strike P.	Bid	Ask	Last Tr.	$ Chg.	Tot. Vol.	Open In.
5	0	0.00	34.05	25.10	27.35	205.00	0.13	0.20	0.22	+0.15	12	148
2	13	-7.43	21.30	19.85	21.70	210.00	0.25	0.34	0.31	+0.16	12	109
14	0	0.00	25.80	15.30	16.95	215.00	0.48	0.56	0.52	+0.35	148	221
27	26	-6.22	13.08	10.85	12.15	220.00	0.91	①1.00	0.94	+0.63	408	514
48	8	-4.82	8.78	7.20	7.80	225.00	1.89	②2.00	1.89	+1.29	369	845
58	153	-4.20	4.25	4.05	4.35	230.00	3.50	③3.80	3.67	+2.27	620	850
329	820	-2.92	2.28	2.00	2.17	235.00	6.45	6.70	6.41	+3.56	340	1236

Do a QPE on the 3 SP's numbered and pick one to trade.

CHART #21: Sell @ 10:45:

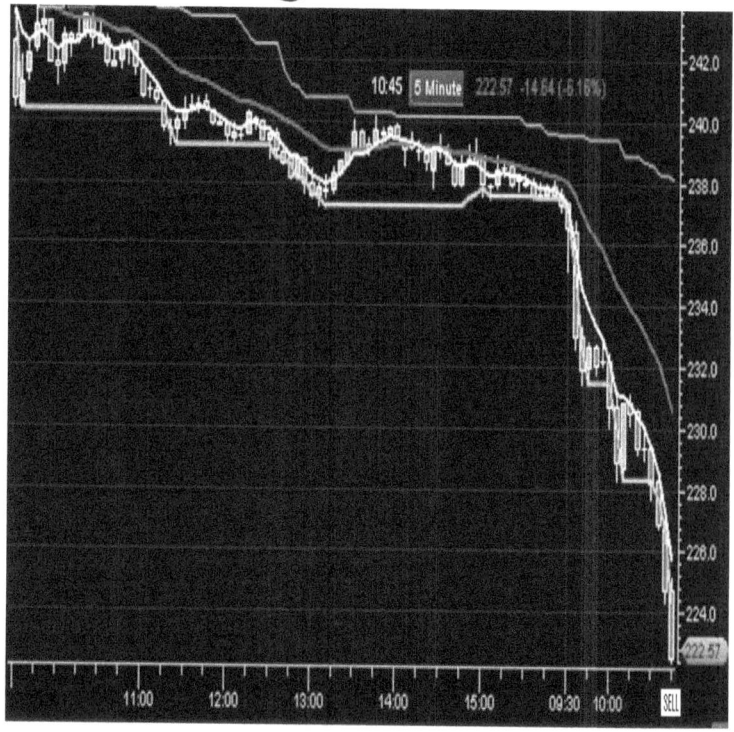

Even though there is NOT a strong indicator to Sell on the 5Min Chart, the Daily Chart had previous Resistance at the same level. The stock dropped to $217 later on, and closed at $222.73. Again, difficult to criticize a 273% profit in 40 minutes (see below).

CHAIN #17: w/CHART #21:

		Calls >				Last 222.57	-14.64 (-6.17%)			< Puts			
Open In	Tot. Vol.	$ Chg.	Last Tr.	Bid	Ask	Strike P.	Bid	Ask	Last Tr.	$ Chg.	Tot. Vol.	Open In
15	3	-13.28	27.22	21.35	25.00	200.00	0.08	0.40	0.39	+0.34	61	102
5	0	0.00	34.05	16.35	20.70	205.00	0.25	1.00	0.75	+0.68	171	148
2	62	-10.51	19.22	12.30	16.00	210.00	0.72	1.71	1.27	+1.12	105	109
14	6	-14.00	11.80	8.55	11.85	215.00	2.06	3.30	1.99	+1.82	660	221
27	75	-11.80	7.50	6.90	7.65	220.00	3.90 SELL	5.00	5.00	+4.69	915	514
48	134	-9.20	4.40	4.00	5.00	225.00	5.30	6.95	5.75	+5.15	1,133	845
58	663	-5.80	2.65	2.40	2.67	230.00	9.40	10.30	9.30	+7.90	1,029	850
329	1,521	-3.85	1.35	1.25	1.45	235.00	13.25	14.15	13.33	+10.48	819	1236

PUT TRADE RESULTS: BUY @ 10:05 – SELL @ 10:45:

SP-220: Buy @ 1.00 x 4 = Risk $414: Sell @ 3.90 = RTN $1546 = Profit +$1132(273%).

SP-225: Buy @ 2.00 x 2 = Risk $412: Sell @ 5.30 = RTN $1048 = Profit +$636 (154%).

SP-230: Buy @ 3.80 x 1 = Risk $391: Sell @ 9.40 = RTN $929 = Profit +$538 (137%).

CHART #22: BUY @ 09:45:

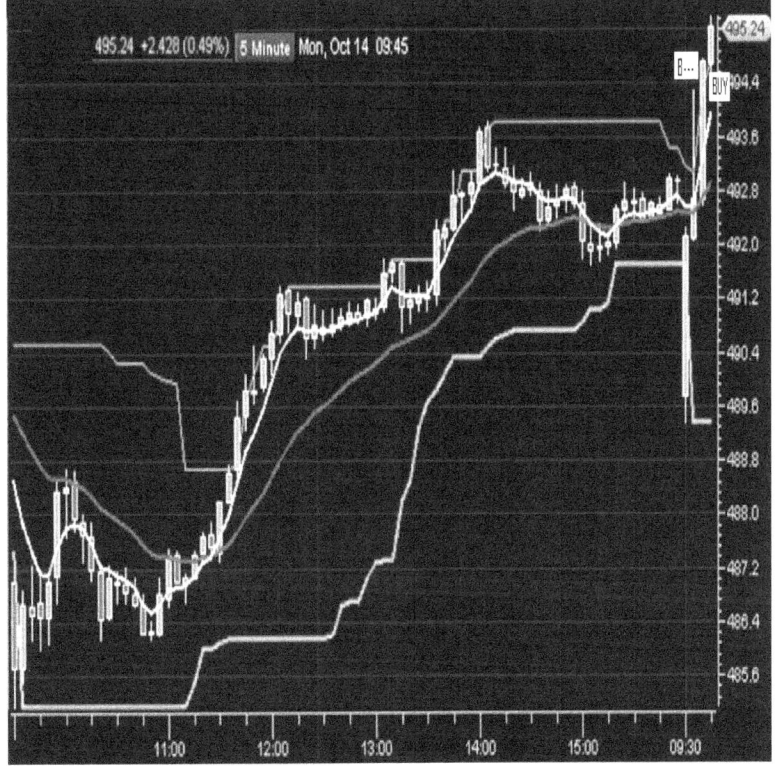

Even after an Open lower than the previous close, a very strong BUY CALL indicator: the 5MA bounced off the 20MA, then headed up with separation; all 4 frames are green; the 3rd frame went higher than the 2nd frame Upper Shadow (B-), and would have also been a very good Buy point; 3rd frame Upper Price Channel Break-out; 4th frame opened above the Upper Price Channel.

CHAIN #18: w/Chart #22 Buy @ 09:45:

Calls >								< Puts			
				Last	495.24	+2.428 (+0.49%)					
Open In	Tot Vol	$ Chg	Last Tr	Bid	Ask	Strike P	Bid	Ask	Last Tr	$ Chg	Tot Vol	Open In
8652	70	+2.00	25.50	25.40	25.90	470.00	0.37	0.38	0.38	-0.09	1,936	12900
6019	99	+2.17	21.00	20.70	21.15	475.00	0.62	0.65	0.63	-0.20	1,686	10020
9461	483	+1.75	16.45	16.25	16.50	480.00	1.12	1.15	1.12	-0.48	2,569	10425
8243	1,322	+1.71	12.31	12.20	12.40	485.00	2.01	2.06	2.00	-0.70	1,574	5895
15968	2,287	+1.25	8.75	8.70	8.85	490.00	3.40	3.50	3.41	-1.09	1,919	11045
13257	3,529	+1.00	5.90	5.80	5.90	495.00	5.50	5.65	5.55	-1.35	1,104	4550
44469	2,861	+0.45	3.60	3.60	3.70	500.00	8.25	8.45	8.30	-1.60	353	15383
10666	2,401	+0.33	2.12	2.11	❶ 2.18	505.00	11.70	12.00	12.00	-1.81	49	1875
22882	1,682	+0.21	1.26	1.24	❷ 1.26	510.00	15.80	16.15	16.02	-2.23	113	9352

Do another QPE but only on 2 SP's (1)(2); pick one to trade. By now you probably realize buying 1 contract is seldom going to have a better Profit potential than buying multiple contracts at a lower premium.

CHART #23: SELL @ 10:05:

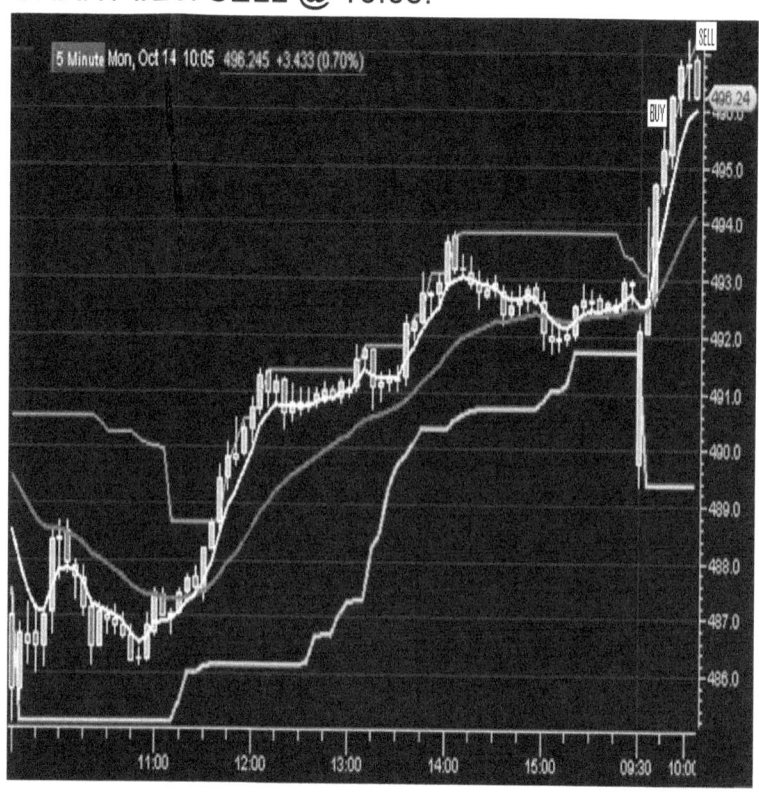

The frame before the Sell frame has an Upper Shadow showing Resistance, and almost no Body which usually indicates a struggle between going up vs down. Adhering to the $$ Management Guideline of not allowing a Net Profit to become a Loss, a SELL is executed. The stock hit a high of $497.58, and closed at $496.04, lower than the Sell.

CHAIN #19: w/CHART#23: SELL @ 10:05:

Calls >						Last 496.245	+3.433 (+0.70%)				< Puts	
Open In.	Tot Vol.	$ Chg.	Last Tr.	Bid	Ask	Strike P.	Bid	Ask	Last Tr.	$ Chg.	Tot Vol.	Open In.
8652	132	+3.88	27.38	26.30	26.85	470.00	0.35	0.37	0.37	-0.10	2,323	12900
6019	172	+3.14	21.97	21.65	22.15	475.00	0.60	0.63	0.59	-0.24	2,846	10020
9461	848	+2.72	17.42	17.15	17.45	480.00	1.05	1.07	1.04	-0.56	4,698	10425
8243	2,182	+2.67	13.27	12.95	13.35	485.00	1.85	1.90	1.87	-0.83	2,408	5895
15968	3,595	+2.15	9.65	9.40	9.60	490.00	3.15	3.30	3.20	-1.30	3,443	11045
13257	5,780	+1.56	6.46	6.35	6.50	495.00	5.15	5.20	5.20	-1.70	2,305	4550
44469	6,581	+0.89	4.04	4.00	4.15	500.00	7.75	7.90	7.80	-2.30	988	15383
10666	5,132	+0.66	2.45	SELL 2.39	2.45	505.00	11.00	11.35	11.04	-2.77	223	1875
22882	4,167	+0.33	1.38	1.35	1.39	510.00	14.95	15.25	15.00	-3.25	162	9352

CALL TRADE RESULTS: BUY @ 09:45 – SELL @ 10:05:

SP-505: Buy @ 2.18 x 2 = Risk $448: Sell @ 2.39 = RTN $466 = Profit +$18 (4%).

SP-510: Buy @ 1.26 x 3 = Risk $391: Sell @ 1.35 = RTN $392 = Profit + $1 (0%).

The trade at SP-505 netted a Profit of $18, or 4%. Before dismissing an $18 Profit, do some quick math. If you NET $18 Profit on 1 trade per day for 1 week, you have a Profit of $90 at the end of the week, which is an 18% gain on a $500 investment fund IN 1 WEEK. If you have an 18% compounded GAIN per week, you will double your investment fund in a little over 4 WEEKS!

CHAPTER #11

USING STOPS

Of the different types of pre-set Stop Orders, OC only uses two. However, we will discuss three types because there is a very important difference between two which must be understood. We'll start with the one STOP OC uses the most.

#1. TRAILING STOP LOSS: this is a pre-set Price value which only TRAILS the BID upward. In other words, every time the Bid moves up, the Trailing Stop Price also moves up to stay within the pre-set value. If the Bid starts to move DOWN, the last Stop Price DOES NOT move down. If the Bid moves down back to the last set Stop Price, a Market Order is triggered. Let's look at an example.

TRAILING STOP LOSS w/ORDER

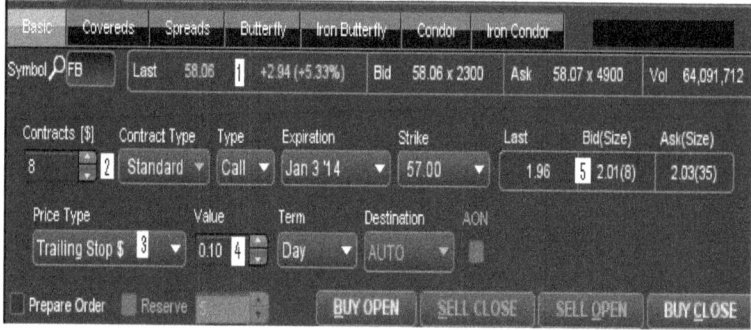

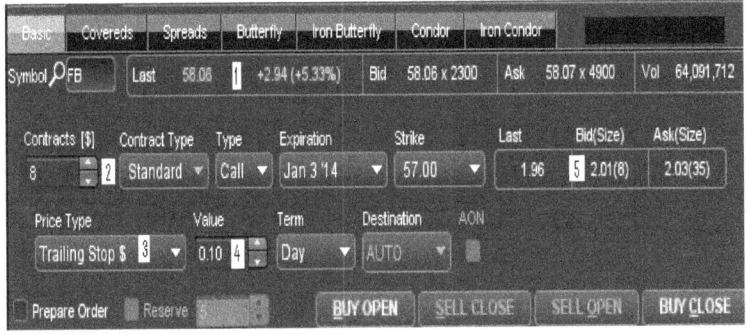

For example, the T.S. Order above shows at (1) the current stock price, the change from the previous Close in price and as a %, and the current Bid, Ask & Volume. At (2) notice the # of contracts, type of option, expiration and Strike Price. At (3) we have the Price Type of the order, in this case, a Trailing Stop $. Notice (4) gives us the Option to set a trailing value, in this case, 0.10. Note: if you set a value (T.S. must be at least 0.10 or greater) which is not allowed, when you go to execute the Order it will not be accepted.

At (5) we see the current BID of 2.01. IMPORTANT: this Trailing Stop with a 0.10 value will have the STOP Price set @ 1.91, which means if the Bid drops to 1.91, a MARKET SELL ORDER is automatically executed. If the BID goes up, for example to 2.05, the Stop Price then moves up to 1.95, which is 0.10 Trailing the Bid. You can always increase the Trailing value, say from 0.10 to 0.15, or whatever you chose.

In order to place the T.S. on an open position, you "SELL CLOSE". Notice the "Confirm Place Order" request which allows you to double check your order, then either "Place" or "Cancel".

If you are going to constantly watch the changing price of your position, you may not want to use the Trailing Stop. You can always move up the Stop Price manually. However, when you get ready to Sell, if you already have in place a Stop Loss Order, you will be able to change it to a Market Order and execute it faster than you can manually enter an Order. As such, your trade will be more effective and convenient.

IMPORTANT: DO NOT MOVE A STOP LOSS DOWN!

STOP LOSS

#2. STOP LOSS: A pre-set price, ($ amount), to close out a transaction which is losing value.

If the price drops to or beneath the Stop Price amount, the order converts to a sell at "market" order. Once again, the price you set must be at least 0.10 beneath current Bid price. If you try to place a Stop Loss which is not allowed, it will not be accepted.

The SL is basically the same as the Trailing Stop, with the exception the Stop Price does NOT move up trailing the bid. However, you can move the SL price yourself at any time.

Every time you move away from your computer, or become distracted from watching the price of your open position, it is strongly recommended you put into place a Stop Loss. Remember, you are dealing with volatile stocks, and as such, they are subject to changing direction immediately.

IMPORTANT: DO NOT MOVE A STOP LOSS DOWN!

STOP LIMIT

#3. STOP LIMIT: A pre-set $ amount to close out a transaction losing value. If the Bid drops under the "Limit", it remains a Limit Order.

This is like a STOP LOSS order with one very big and crucial difference: if the Bid drops beneath your set Stop Limit Price, it DOES NOT trigger an immediate Sell at Market Order.

The Stop Limit remains set at the price and only triggers if the price is quoted. For Example: you set a Stop Limit at 1.10. However, the stock drops quickly, and the Option Bid drops from 1.13 to 1.09, skipping over a bid of 1.10. The Stop Limit @ 1.10 remains a Limit Order. If the Option Bid Price DOES NOT hit on 1.10, the Limit Sell order DOES NOT execute. If the Price keeps dropping, you keep losing money unless you manually change the Order. OC DOES NOT use Stop Limit Orders.

OPTIONS COURSE PART #12

PAPER TRADING & TOOLS

"Paper Trading" is strongly recommended. If you don't have an account with a Broker, there are sites which offer free stock and option quotes, with continuous updates. Check with Discount Brokers because some of them allow you to open an account WITHOUT funding it, and "paper trade" for a limited period of time.

If you have an account, learn and practice utilizing the charts, chains, tools, etc. Even though Brokers might share common streaming data, their Trading Platforms will have differences in the way they are presented and navigated. Paper Trading is the time to become familiar with the Trading Platform you will be using, and the tools available.

Create a Watch List. Decide if you want to "day trade", or "swing trade" (buy and hold an option for more than one day). Practice chart reading and start predicting (on paper) stock moves noting time and price. Use both the Daily and Minutes charts looking for trends and resistance. Then start matching your stock predictions with the applicable Option Chains, and start making Paper option buys (use ask) and sells (use bid).

Paper Trading Example

Example: 07/20 Friday: 10:40

BIDU: 109.7: <u>BUY</u> Jy/20 CALL 110 @ .67x 4 = -281 Risk

………10:50 @ 110.7: @ 1.05 (bid) (Stop Loss @ .90)

………11:10 @ 111.1: @ 1.27 (Trailing Stop @ .20)

<u>SOLD</u> 11:15 @ 110.9 @ 1.05/MKT x4 = 407 (+126) 45%

(T.S. @1.07 trigger)

Think in percentages (%'s). Say BIDU above was the only trade for the day and had SOLD at .85: x4 = 327 = +$46. Whereas $46 does not seem like a great profit (fees were $26), the trade made 16% on the Risk; and 5% on an Investment Fund of $500 in one day. If you make a profit +$46 a day, you will double your I.F. in 11 trading days.

Study your gains and losses. The most common mistakes: buying too early; NOT taking a small loss; NOT taking profits; not looking for points of resistance. When you start to make $$ on paper, you're ready to start trading with real $$.

REMEMBER: Paper Trading mistakes do not lose real $$.

TOOLS:

There are 3 basic TOOLS which OC has developed to make certain calculations easier and faster for you to perform. As part of this Course we are listing the formulas used for each TOOL. However, if you go to the OC website, you will be able to access the TOOL itself where you will only have to insert #'s, and not have to do the math functions to get results.

TOOLS: DEFINITION & FORMULA

Examples USING $10 per trade cost and $1 per contract cost.

#1. Fees: cost above option premium needed to do the trade.

TRADE COST + (CONTRACT COST x # OF CONTRACTS) = FEES. Buy 5 contracts: 10 + 5(1x5) = $15 trade fees. Sell fees would be same $15. Total trade fees Round Trip (buy & sell) would be $30.

#2. Break Even: the amount of option premium gain needed to pay for Fees.

Buy 5 contracts: (Trade Cost divided by # of contracts + cost of 1 contract) divided by 100 x2 =

needed gain amount. (10 divided by 5 + 1) divided by 100 x2 = .06. Option price needs to gain .06 to break even. If you had bought 5 contracts at $1, you need the premium to go up to 1.06 to break even: Buy 5 @ $1 = $500 + $10 trade cost + $1 per contract (x5) = total Risk of $515 + Sell cost of $15 (sell trade $10 + $1 per contract) = needed return of $530 to break even: divided by 5 contracts = .06 gain.

#3. Quick Profit Estimate (QPE): determines Strike Price profit potential.

To calculate the QPE: CALL: subtract the SP Ask premium from the Bid of the next LOWER level strike price (deeper ITM, or closer to ITM), which will equal an estimate return per contract; then multiply by the number of contracts you can Buy at the Ask.

PUT: subtract the SP Ask premium from the Bid of the next HIGHER level strike price (deeper ITM, or closer to ITM), which will equal an estimate return per contract; then multiply by the number of contracts you can Buy at the Ask. See example in Chapter#10, Part #1.

CHAPTER #13

SUMMARY

#1. Use good Money management.

#2. Take a profit.

#3. Limit and take a loss.

#4. Follow the Charts.

#5. Call Options: buy for stock price to go up.

#6. Put Options: buy for stock price to go down.

#7. Options have 3 end results:

(a). Exercise the Option and convert to stock.

(b). Sell for a profit or loss.

(c). Expiration.

#8. A standard Option contract controls 100 shares of stock. Multiply price x 100.

#9. CALL In The Money (ITM): Stock price is higher than Strike price.

#10.PUT In The Money (ITM): Stock price is lower than Strike price.

#11. Option Premium requirements:

(a). CALL: The Ask price must be equal to or greater than the STOCK price MINUS the STRIKE price.

(b). PUT: The ask price must be equal to or greater than the STRIKE price MINUS the STOCK price.

#12. Time value is worthless @ expiration.

#13. The 3 big $$$ making ?s are:

(a). What direction will stock move?

(b). Which Option to buy?

(c). Will the Option make $$$?

#12. Think in percentages, not just dollar amounts.

#13. Type of Stops:

(a). STOP LIMIT: If Bid drops under the "Limit" price, it remains a Limit Order and will not execute until Price is bid quoted.

(b). STOP LOSS: If the price drops beneath the Stop price, the order converts to a "market" order and executes.

(c). TRAILING STOP: set a value which trails the bid up, but does not move down. If set price is hit, Trailing Stop converts to Market order.

#14. Stock criteria:

(a). DAILY VOLUME AVERAGE: pick stocks trading more than 1/2 Million shares a day. Greater volume = greater option volatility.

(b). VOLATILITY: due to short term trading, a stock needs to move in price (gain/loss) at least 10% (or 5% on high $ stocks) 2-3 times every 60 trade days. Volatility equals good chart trends.

(c). CHART TREND: look for multiple tops and bottoms, Cross-Overs, Volatility, and confirming moves.

(d).. NEWS: pay attention to events especially earnings.

~~

A note from the Author:

Thank you for taking the time to learn this simple investment strategy. At the very least, you now should have a much greater understanding of Stock Options than before. As one student said after being tutored, this Course "de-mystified options" for him. Even if you do not start trading options now, there is always the chance you might start later on. Congratulations on taking another step toward financial success.

ABOUT THE AUTHOR

The Author currently resides in California and trades options from the comfort of his home office. He tutors individuals groups, and companies. For group seminars, or helping your company start options investing for itself, contact:
pleasemailshawn@gmail.com

DISCLAIMER

The purpose of this book is educational only. This book is not a recommendation to buy or sell, but rather contains guidelines in re interpreting various analytical tools and methods. All information should only be used by investors who are fully aware of the risks inherent in any and all stock market trading. Although every effort has been made to ensure the accuracy of the information contained in this book, there may be errors, both typographical and factual. This book is presented with the understanding the author and publisher are not providing financial, legal, or other professional advice or services, and accept no liability whatsoever for any gain or loss arising from the use of this book.

www.ingramcontent.com/pod-product-compliance
Lightning Source LLC
Chambersburg PA
CBHW071753170526
45167CB00003B/1017